Heartland RISING

The Defense of American Values

By Martin Capages Jr. PhD

© 2021 MARTIN CAPAGES JR.

All rights reserved. No part of this book may be reproduced or utilized in any form or by any means, electronic or mechanical, including photocopying, recording or by any information storage retrieval system without permission in writing from the publisher, except for a reviewer who may quote brief passages in a review to be printed in a newspaper, magazine or electronic publication.

American Freedom Publications LLC

www.americanfreedompublications.com

2638 E. Wildwood Road

Springfield 65804

ISBN 978-1-63752-370-4 Paperback Version

ISBN 978-1-63752-371-1 eBook Version

Cover Design: Christopher. M. Capages

www.capagescreative.com

First Edition-April 15, 2021

Printed in the United States of America

THE BEST DEFENSE IS A GOOD OFFENSE
-Carl von Clausewitz

DEDICATION

To Rush Limbaugh -An American Heartland Patriot

"There is good in everything that happens if you look for it."

---Rush Limbaugh

HEARTLAND RISING

TABLE OF CONTENTS

DEDICATION iv
PREFACE 7
THE AMERICAN HEARTLAND 11
AMERICAN HEARTLAND VALUES 17
    SIX BASIC AMERICAN CULTURAL VALUES 17
        Individual Freedom and Self-Reliance 18
        Equality of Opportunity and Competition 21
        The American Dream and Hard Work 23
"INSURRECTION" 25
THE RETURN OF OBAMANATION 30
THE FIVE BIG LIES 34
BIG LIE NO. 1 "SYSTEMIC RACISM" 37
        FROM CAMBRIDGE TO CHARLOTTESVILLE 38
BIG LIE NO. 2 "CATASTROPHIC CLIMATE CHANGE" 48
BIG LIE NO. 3 "THE GREEN NEW DEAL" 53
BIG LIE NO. 4 "HEALTHCARE IS A RIGHT" 59
BIG LIE NO. 5 "CHINA IS NOT OUR COMPETITOR" 65
DEFENDING AMERICAN VALUES 72
    THE MAINSTREAM MEDIA 72
    FREEDOM OF THE PRESS 73
    BIG TECH 76
    FREE SPEECH 86
    THE RIGHT TO BEAR ARMS 89

PREPARING FOR 2022 and 2024 91
    2018 HEALTHCARE MISSTEP 91
    2020 MISSTEPS 93
    THE COVID 19 PANDEMIC 93
    MAIL-IN VOTING 98
    SUBURBAN WOMEN VOTE 103
    THE BLACK EXIT. WHERE WAS IT? 103
    HEALTHCARE 105
    CLIMATE CHANGE 105
    MAINSTREAM MEDIA BIAS AND BIG TECH 106
    DEFENDING THE SECOND AMMENDMENT 106
    BUT WHAT ABOUT IMMIGRATION REFORM? 106
THE BIG PICTURE 108
SUMMARY OF ACTION PLAN 110
REFERENCES AND WORKS CITED 111
ABOUT THE AUTHOR 113

PREFACE

The American Heartland has had ***enough*** and it is going to do something about it in 2022 and 2024. Let's be clear, the United States of America is a great country. To most Americans, it is the greatest country in the World. It was founded on Judeo-Christian principles and became a free nation in 1776. It corrected its major flaw, the slavery of blacks in 1865. It wasn't a perfect correction. It took the courage of a black pastor, Dr. Martin Luther King Jr. to peacefully protest and achieve what was written in 1776, "We hold these truths to be self-evident, that all men are created equal, that they are endowed by their Creator with certain unalienable Rights, that among these are Life, Liberty and the pursuit of Happiness."

People in the American Heartland are not racist, and they are through being called that by the media, celebrities and political elites. They believe that All Lives Matter to their Creator and that the Black Lives Matter movement is Marxist blather and evil in its intent.

The Heartland rejects the onslaught of fascists calling themselves Antifa. They are the obvious brown shirts of the Democratic Party since there was no outcry from that party during the violent protests and riots during 2020 and there has been no effort by Federal law enforcement to arrest the leaders and organizers of those local insurrections. Catch and release is not law enforcement. Politicians like Kamala Harris paying the legal fees of looters is, in itself, near criminal. And yes, those BLM/Antifa riots were actual insurrections against the Rule of Law. Federal property was damaged, civilians and police were killed and over 2000 law enforcement officers were injured. A retired police captain, David Dorn, was fatally shot during a BLM/Antifa inspired looting while he was protecting a friend's property in St. Louis. Captain Dorn had been a father of five and had 10 grandchildren. He had been passionate about helping young people, but BLM didn't care.

PREFACE

The event of January 6, 2021 at the Nation's capitol *was not an insurrection*. It was a social media-fueled protest that was hijacked by a few individuals. To call that an insurrection while ignoring the damage done by BLM and Antifa all summer 2020 and *even as it continues in Portland, Oregon* is disingenuous. To place the Capitol behind razor wire with National Guard troops on the perimeter is an over-reaction and political theater. Hunting down those few Capitol protestors while ignoring the large number of BLM/Antifa protest organizers has been a departure from Equal Justice under the Law. And it has not gone unnoticed by the Heartland.

The nation's law enforcement and intelligence agencies have lost credibility with We the People as a result of the Russian Collusion hoax initiated by those very agencies. Fifty of those past agency heads even tried to cover up the dubious activity of the Biden family captured on Hunter Biden's laptop by issuing a statement saying it was all "Russian disinformation." The old saying, *"fool me once shame on you, fool me twice, shame on me"* comes to mind. A two-tier legal system is not going to be tolerated and the rejection will come in 2022 at the ballot box. And these ballots will be watched closely. That will set the table for 2024.

The initial days of the Biden Administration have been an affront to the American Heartland. In his shallow election campaign, former VP Joseph Biden bragged that he would be the most "Progressive President in history." Progressivism is Socialism. During the campaign when asked by George Stephanopoulos about the use of executive orders to legislate what he said he believed should require approval from Congress, his response was *"No, well, I've gotta get the votes. I gotta get the votes. That's why — you know, the one thing that I — I have this strange notion. We are a democracy. Some of my Republican friends and some of my Democratic friends even occasionally say, 'Well, if you can't get the votes, by executive order you're going to do something.' Things you can't do by executive order unless you're a dictator.*

We're a democracy. We need consensus." He was right but he didn't mean it in his heart.

His first order of business was to issue a barrage of Executive Orders that undid positive actions of his predecessor, Donald Trump. With a great flourish, he would cancel the Keystone XL pipeline, forcing thousands of Americans out of work, including thousands of highly-skilled union jobs. It was just stupid. The American refineries need the heavy crude from Canada and now it will be shipped by trucks and railcars. Next, he would undo the positive border and immigration action taken by the Trump administration. This will have terrible consequences. The health and social security systems supported by American citizens will be overwhelmed by the influx of illegal aliens and crime rates will increase. National security will be more difficult to achieve with no checks at the open border. There will be an influx of terrorists. They will blend in with the flow of "undocumented immigrants."

After his senseless Executive Orders, he would then appoint nearly all of the known corrupt officials of the past Obama/Biden Administration to important roles, to include Susan Rice, an individual that openly lied to the American people on broadcast media five times in one day. She would now push "equity" not "equality." This would be followed by the appointment of John Kerry as Climate Czar, nearly the most misinformed politician of all time with the exception of perhaps, Biden himself as evidenced by his initial actions. Biden would tout the diversity of his cabinet appointees, not competency or relevant experience. They had none. It was the color of their skin, gender or sexual orientation, not their character that mattered. Even before completing his first 100 days, Biden has set back American race relations 100 years.

PREFACE

It is very apparent that President Biden and the Democratic Party did not understand the message of the 2016 Presidential Election or the 2010 Tea Party. Their focus was, and continues to be, on the negative personality traits of the Messenger, Donald Trump and not the Message itself. It was the Trump Administration policies under the banners Make America Great Again and America First that most of the Nation supported with near unanimous support in the American Heartland. Trump's agenda resonated with the very essence of Heartland values, Individual Freedom, Equality of Opportunity and The American Dream.

It is also very apparent that the mainstream media have failed in their duty to be objective reporters. They do not need to be patriots. They just need to be honest and they haven't been for a long time. It may be too late for the media to return to the Journalist Creed. If they remain corrupt, they can watch as the American Heartland rises to do its duty at the ballot box in 2022.

Martin Capages Jr. PhD
American Freedom Publications LLC

THE AMERICAN HEARTLAND

The United States of America is a polarized nation. It is split between two factions. One faction is guided by Common Sense. The other faction relies on Emotion. These factions are inherent in the human condition and the United States is not immune.

There is a need for some Emotion. Common Sense can be extremely boring and interest in a singular subject can, and will, fade rapidly. Emotion, on the other hand, grabs the attention of the masses. It doesn't matter if it is fact or fiction, truth or lies, or even rationality or insanity. The era of the Trump Administration brought both of these factions to the surface. Unfortunately for the Nation, there has been only one predominate viewpoint driven by the mainstream media, a viewpoint that was blurred by a singular Emotion, a visceral hatred for President Trump.

In the 2016 Presidential election, the Heartland made itself known by choosing a populist outsider to be the Chief Executive, Donald J. Trump. This election went contrary to the establishment in Washington D. C., nicknamed "The Swamp" and brought dismay to the mainstream media. President Trump had won through the Electoral College but lost the popular vote by less than three million votes. The outcome was decided by the swing states in the Midwest "rust belt" and the residual Tea Party voters in the Heartland. The establishment, coastal elites and mainstream media would be in complete denial. The fact that nearly half the voting population disagreed with their Progressive values was ignored. The new President would be attacked with an emotional fervor which was unprecedented. It even exceeded the venomous onslaught against George W. Bush.

Emotion sells. It is the bread and butter of the legacy media and the new digital social media. While it may seem strange that Pulitzer prizes are being awarded for false reporting as exemplified by the Russian Collusion hoax, it has become the Standard of Practice for the New York Times, the Washington Post, CNN, NBC, ABC, CBS, MSNBC, PBS and NPR. The false reporting resulted in the destruction of the populist President. The clash of medias was apparent in Twitter and Facebook's censorship of the New York Post's article on the corruption of the Biden family revealed in the dealings of Hunter Biden with Russia, the Ukraine and China.

The hypocrisy of the main stream media, Big Tech, Hollywood, coastal elites and the Democratic Party was so obvious that it was apparently not "newsworthy." This lineup of characters had identified their enemy, Donald J. Trump and his supporters in the American Heartland. The Heartland does exist, but it is disorganized. It is split between conservatives (most Republicans), the military, veterans and police as well as the more moderate Democrats and Independents made up of rural folks and the trade union rank and file (not the union leadership).

Recent elections and political rhetoric seem to indicate that the dangers of socialism and communism have been forgotten. The students on the college and university campuses are doing what students seem to always do, join the latest, heart-pulling liberal cause. They are open to ideas that they are told are new and beneficial to all of humanity. One of these "new" ideas is Democratic Socialism. The students need to examine the sources of the information and research the actual history. The results are clear. Socialism always fails. The "Democratic Socialism" promoted by Alexandria Ocasio-Cortez and her Squad, Bernie Sanders and now the center plank of the Democratic Party is the anti-thesis of Freedom and Liberty.

What is the heartland of America? Some say that Heartland is an American political term referring to U.S. states that "don't touch an ocean," whether the Atlantic or Pacific, or perhaps it is a reference to the Midwestern United States. But the Heartland is not just the land between the coasts or what elitists call "flyover country." It is not just the red areas on the map that show the 2016 and 2020 Presidential election results of the Electoral College or the popular vote in each county [or parish]. Most of the U. S. population resides on the coasts and the major metropolitan centers. Flyover Country is sparsely populated representing only a small portion of the Heartland. The major portion of the Heartland population resides in the small suburban communities that are on the fringes of the larger cities.

The "Heartlanders" are low to middle incomers, have their kids enrolled in public, faith-based or independent charter schools. Some even home-school their kids. For years, the typical Heartland family had one parent working and the other parent staying at home with the pre-school kids. This has only changed in recent years when economics made two income families a necessity and daycare a requirement. This has been detrimental to the concept of the "nuclear family", the main strength of Heartland.

Most Heartlanders are American citizens by birth, but their grandparents may have been immigrants. They practice their faith, coach basketball and soccer camps, watch little leaguers, football mighty-mites, and basketball. Most of the Heartlanders work for someone else but there are some small business owners as well. They feel the effects of inflation and increasing energy prices. The local police and other first responders are heroes to Heartlanders. Their political leanings are based more on family tradition than on party platforms. Very few Heartlanders participate in government public service. Many public-school teachers would be Heartlanders, but they are controlled by the far-left Teachers Union leadership. [Public sector unions should be illegal anyway.]

THE AMERICAN HEARTLAND

The Heartland has become very susceptible to propaganda due to its historical trust in the traditional mainstream media and a naivete regarding internet social media platforms. It continues to be easily manipulated due to its belief in the inherent good of people. It believes its elected officials are all patriots and each of those officials has the desire to sacrificially provide service to the Nation without financial gain. It is a belief that has been betrayed by the Democratic Party whose only desire is to gain absolute power and enhance their own wealth and prestige. It has also been betrayed by the lack of due diligence and political naivete of the Republican Party.

The COVID-19 Pandemic of 2020 was used to good effect by the Democratic Party to use mail-in voting and information suppression to eek-out the successful election of an aging, incompetent and corrupt professional politician, Joe Biden. The media would use the Pandemic to shelter Biden from interviews that would reveal the actual objective of the Democratic Party, the return of Obamanation, the divisive, misguided policies of President Barack Obama.

The Presidential Election of 2020 was characterized by a willingness to win the Executive office regardless of the means, to include tacit support of street riots, vandalism and judicial activism. The Democrats were helped by President Trump's continued narcissism, placing himself in the center of every controversy, delegating properly but then co-opting the delegate. His use of "I" instead of "We" would lead to his decline in favor among the suburban elites and provide ammunition for a deranged mainstream media. It was clear that he would need to win the election by a substantial amount to stave off the mail-in ballot fraud mechanism set in place by Democrats at the state and county levels. [One pollster would even say as much.] He would garner ten million more votes than he did in the last election but would somehow lose to an opponent who would get even more votes than mathematical logic would support. The swing states would all go blue as the ballots were counted until the Democrats prevailed. The return to Obamanation would then begin in earnest.

The new President's selection of Cabinet and other officials has shown a deafness to the Heartland's cry for a return to morality in government. The Heartland has just recently developed a distrust of establishment motives but has always had a deep loathing for the big city values exhibited by major Democrat controlled cities and states. These morally decadent values are a cancer called Progressivism that is metastasizing and will be followed by a slide into Statism, Socialism and Communism if not resisted. But a resistance is building in the American Heartland.

Of course, the Nation's situation is much more complicated than this. And unfortunately, its survival is now on the line. Will Emotion continue to be the driver of public thought or will the Common Sense of the American Heartland rise to the challenge and save the Nation from itself?

AMERICAN HEARTLAND VALUES

Individual Freedom

Equality of Opportunity

The American Dream

AMERICAN HEARTLAND VALUES

In my first book, *The Moral Case for American Freedom*, I put forth the premise that the American way of life, including its governing philosophy of Individual Freedom, was derived from Judeo-Christian beliefs. This governing philosophy was built into the Declaration of Independence and the Constitution of the United States. It is clear from these basic documents that individual rights are from a divine source above the State. All elected officials and military personnel take an oath to protect that Constitution from all enemies, foreign and domestic.

But America is also built on cultural values. One of the best descriptions of these values was developed by Vintage American Ways. Their stated mission is "Reminding Americans that our basic American values, which unite us all, are far greater than anything that divides us." It is hard to disagree with that. (Six Basic American Cultural Values, 2021) The following is an adaptation of Vintage American Ways material:

SIX BASIC AMERICAN CULTURAL VALUES

This description of American cultural values, the six basic American cultural values, was first introduced in *American Ways: An Introduction to American Culture*. It explains the value system that has allowed the United States to assimilate millions of people from diverse cultures all over the world and create a unique, enduring American identity. "There are three pairs of values consisting of three reasons why immigrants have come (and still do) to the United States and three prices that are paid for these benefits. The values and prices paid to achieve these values are:

Individual Freedom and Self-Reliance
Equality of Opportunity and Competition
The American Dream and Hard Work

AMERICAN HEARTLAND VALUES

The first value is Individual Freedom and the price for that is Self-Reliance. We cannot be truly free if we cannot take care of ourselves and be independent. The second value is Equality of Opportunity, and the price for that is Competition. If everyone has an equal chance for success, then we have to compete. The third value is The American Dream, the opportunity for a better life and a higher standard of living. The price for the American Dream has traditionally been Hard Work."

These six basic cultural values describe the American Heartland. They are contrary to the concepts of "equity" and "social justice" that have been embraced by the far-left Democratic Socialist wing of Democratic Party. It is a matter of the Power of the State versus Individual Freedom.

Individual Freedom and Self-Reliance

The earliest settlers came to the North American continent to establish colonies that were free from the controls that existed in European societies. They wanted to escape the controls placed on many aspects of their lives by kings and governments, priests and churches, noblemen and aristocrats. To a great extent, they succeeded. In 1776, the British colonial settlers declared their independence from England and established a new nation, the United States of America. In so doing, they defied the king of England and declared that the power to govern would lie in the hands of the people.

Freed from the power of the King, they wrote a constitution for their new nation that separated church and state so that there would never be a government-supported church. Also, in this new Constitution they expressly forbade titles of nobility to ensure that an aristocratic society would not develop. There would be no ruling class of noblemen in the new nation. But unfortunately, an aristocracy of sorts would develop in the South.

The agrarian economy of the South was pre-industrial and slavery was the unfortunate result. It would take a Civil War to ensure that Individual Freedom was for all Individuals. That was a correction in the moral values of the Nation. Cultural values are different, but both moral values and cultural values are the foundation of our democratic nation. Rooted in the beliefs and visions of our Founding Fathers and reinforced by historical experience, these cultural values are what distinguishes our country from all others. They are what make us "Americans."

> *"We hold these truths to be self-evident, that all men are created equal, that they are endowed by their Creator with certain inalienable rights, that among these are Life, Liberty and the pursuit of Happiness."*
> *The Declaration of Independence (1776)*

By freedom, Americans mean the desire and the right of all individuals to control their own destiny without outside interference from the government, a ruling noble class, the church, or any other organized authority, **or person**.

There is, however, a cost for this benefit of *individual freedom*. That cost is the requirement for *self-reliance*. Individuals must learn to rely on themselves or risk losing freedom. They must take responsibility for themselves. Traditionally, this has meant achieving both financial and emotional independence from their parents as early as possible, usually by age eighteen or twenty-one. Self-reliance means that Americans believe they should take care of themselves, solve their own problems, and "stand on their own two feet."

Charles-Louis de Secondat, Baron de La Brède et de Montesquieu, was a French lawyer, man-of-letters and political philosopher who lived during the Age of Enlightenment. He is famous for his articulation of the theory of Separation of Powers, which is implemented in many constitutions throughout the world, including our own. One of his most famous works is *The Spirit of the Laws* that was published anonymously in France in 1748 and then translated and published in English in 1750. Montesquieu spent over twenty years researching and writing *The Spirit of the Laws* since it covered such a wide range of subjects such as the law, social life and even the study of anthropology. In this political treatise, Montesquieu pleaded in favor of a constitutional system of government and the separation of powers, the ending of slavery, the preservation of civil liberties and the law, and the idea that political institutions ought to reflect the social and geographical aspects of each community.

Count Alexis de Tocqueville, applied Montesquieu's methods to a study of American society in his work *Democracy in America*. His *Democracy in America* was published in 1835 after Tocqueville's travels in the United States and is today considered an early work of sociology and political science.

As Americans, it is hard not to like Tocqueville. He was upbeat in his observations of the progress the young United States of America was making towards democracy. Today feminists would take offense at some of his opinions. But Tocqueville was also worried about mistakes America could make and issued warnings about the "Tyranny of the Majority".

He was prejudiced in many ways as well, but who isn't? He believed in liberty and individual freedom while respecting the rights of others. Of centralized government, he wrote that it *"excels in preventing, not doing."* On liberty he wrote, *"I have a passionate love for liberty, law, and respect for rights"*, and, *"I am neither of the revolutionary party nor of the conservative.... Liberty is my foremost passion."*

Tocqueville observed the Americans' belief in self-reliance in the 1830s:

> *"They owe nothing to any man, they expect nothing from any man; they acquire the habit of always considering themselves as standing alone, and they are apt to imagine that their whole destiny is in their own hands."*

This strong belief in self-reliance continues today as a traditional American value. It is perhaps one of the most difficult aspects of the American character to understand, but it is profoundly important. Most Americans believe that they must be self-reliant in order to keep their freedom. If they rely too much on the support of their families or the government or any organization, they may lose some of their freedom to do what they want. In order to be in the mainstream of American life, they must be seen as truly self-reliant.

Most Americans still believe in the value of *hard work*. This cultural inclination will be discussed later in this chapter, but it means that most Americans believe that people should hold jobs and not live off welfare payments from the government. There have been many efforts to reform the welfare system so that people would not become dependent on welfare and stop looking for jobs to support themselves.

Equality of Opportunity and Competition

American values such as equality of opportunity and self-reliance are ideals that may not necessarily describe the reality of American life. Equality of opportunity, for example, is an ideal that is not always put into practice. Some people will always have a better chance for success than others. Those who are born into rich families have more opportunities than those who are born into poorer families. Inheriting money does give a person a decided advantage. Race and gender may still be factors affecting success, although there are laws designed to promote equality of opportunity for all individuals. And, of course, new immigrants continue to face challenges unique to their situation. Generations of immigrants have come to the United States with the belief that everyone has a chance to succeed here. They have felt that because individuals are free from excessive political, religious, and social controls, they have a better chance for personal success. Many found that they did indeed have a better chance to succeed in the United States than in their old country. Because millions of these immigrants succeeded, Americans have come to believe in equality of opportunity. When Tocqueville visited the United States in the 1830s, he was impressed by the great uniformity of conditions of life in the new nation. He wrote,

> *"The more I advanced in the study of American society, the more I perceived that . . . equality of condition is the fundamental fact from which all others seem to be derived."*

It is important to understand what most Americans mean when they say they believe in equality of opportunity. They do not mean that everyone is—or should be—equal. That is not equality, that is equity. Equity is found in Socialism and Communism. And unfortunately, it is the guiding philosophy of the Biden Administration. It is a forced uniformity that is enforced by a dictatorship of the Elite, a group of competitive, but cooperative, political and financial oligarchies.

The actual American meaning of Equality is Equality of Opportunity. Each individual should have an equal chance for success. Americans see much of life as a race for success. For them, equality means that everyone should have an equal chance to enter the race and win. In other words, equality of opportunity may be thought of as an ethical rule. It helps ensure that the race for success is a fair one and that a person does not win just because he or she was born into a wealthy family. And should not lose because of their race or religion.

This American concept of "fair play" is an important aspect of the belief in equality of opportunity.

President Abraham Lincoln expressed this belief in the 1860s when he said,

> *"We ... wish to allow the humblest man an equal chance to get rich with everybody else. When one starts poor, as most do in the race of life, free society is such that he knows he can better his condition; he knows that there is no fixed condition of labor for his whole life."*

However, the price to be paid for this equality of opportunity is competition. If much of life is seen as a race, then a person must run the race in order to succeed. A person has the responsibility to compete with others, even though not everyone will win the race. But, it is every person's duty to try to win on their own, without outside assistance.

The American Dream and Hard Work

The distance between the very wealthy, called the 1% and the rest of the population has dramatically increased as a result of the 2020 COVID-19 Pandemic. Still, most Americans believe in the ideal of the American Dream that if they work hard, their lives, and more importantly, their children's lives will be better.

Americans in the Heartland believe that people should hold jobs and not live off welfare payments from the government. This is contrary to the values of the major cities and states under Democrat control. Staying in power requires passing out "free stuff", no strings attached. Therefore, the leadership of these cities and states continue to resist efforts by conservatives to reform the welfare system with incentives to seek work or training opportunities.

As the United States has shifted from an industry-based economy to one that is service or information-based, there has been a decline in high-paying jobs for factory workers. As the United States competes in a global economy, many workers are losing their old jobs and finding that they and their family members must now work longer hours for less money and fewer benefits.

When the economy weakens, everyone suffers, and there are greater numbers of the working poor—those who work hard but have low-paying jobs that do not provide a decent standard of living and may not provide health insurance and retirement benefits, and many must rely on some outside assistance, from the government or other sources.

One of the contributing factors to the decline in the middle-class has been the mis-match of college and university curriculums with economic reality. Technology has increased exponentially while the tenured far-left leaning college and university faculties have either embraced societal and political course curriculums or succumbed to government research grants with political, not public interest goals. It is not clear if this is ideology-driven or just educational laziness.

There have been significant increases in courses on information technology applications, but not the underlying science of computer technology or machine-level programming software. However, the shortfall has been filled by the community technical colleges to some extent. We need to be thankful for that. Unfortunately, technical colleges attract little government or alumni funding since they lack the prestige of traditional four-year brick and mortar, ivy covered colleges and universities. The theory that on-line education would level the playing field may turn out to be a correct axiom, but the level playing field will produce less qualified graduates for real world requirements.

Overall, the Democratic Party mantra that everyone wants "a good paying union job" shows a leadership stuck in the last century. The unions represent less than eight percent of the American work force. A union job is not the American Dream today.

"INSURRECTION"

On his first day in office, following a speech that emphasized the need for National unity, President Joseph R. Biden, Jr. set about to divide the Nation further by signing a suite of Executive Orders that undid the positive effects of the Trump administration. It was an intentional thumb in the eye of nearly seventy-five million Americans and defied logic. In fact, it was worse than that, his Executive Orders were stupid and spilling over with hatred for the middle class in the American Heartland.

That hatred would be brazenly exhibited by the petulant Speaker of the House, Nancy Pelosi who would continue the attack on Heartland values with another impeachment trial of a President *who had already left office.* She would add fuel to the fire by appointing partisan trial managers who had openly lied to the American people during the first impeachment, Adam Schiff, Jerry Nadler and Eric Swalwell. The incoming new President would do nothing to tamp done the fraudulent and wasteful Democrat rebuke of the Constitution.

The only thing that Joe Biden had in common with his predecessor was that he seemed intent on keeping some of his own campaign promises, but those would be the ones that would divide the Nation further. Unfortunately, his campaign promises were not widely known due to the shelter provided by a complicit mainstream media and Big Tech. Big Tech not only censured possible dissenting opinions but also made major contributions to the Democratic Party. Wall Street, 'woke' major Corporations and Hollywood elites also kicked in heart-stopping amounts of cash. Much of this went to the mail-in ballot effort and the funding of numerous legal challenges to individual state election laws in the swing states. Many unconstitutional actions were taken by state election officials, both naïve Republicans and partisan Democrats.

Because of this seemingly unusual election process (the first time that a large number mail-in ballots were used for a Presidential election), there were questions that went unanswered. Social media was employed to garner a protest at the Capitol on January 6th, the day Congress was to certify the individual State electoral votes. Objections to certain State electors, in accordance with the U. S. Constitution, were to be offered on the floor by several Senators, but there was a delay due to the unfortunate disruption of the process by a fringe group of protestors who hijacked the protest from the larger group of peaceful demonstrators and then forced their way into the Capitol building. Unfortunately, a Capitol policeman died and one unarmed protestor was killed as a direct result of the protest. The New York Times promoted the claim that the Capitol policeman, Brian Sicknick was bludgeoned to death with a fire-extinguisher. *This was untrue.* After being part of the security force during the actions at the Capitol on January 6th, he went back to his office. Some hours later, he collapsed and then later died. The cause of death is under investigation. The sole protestor who was killed was Air Force veteran Ashli Babbitt. Babbitt was shot dead by an on-duty officer who has remained unnamed for several weeks after the incident. But the Democratic Party would make use of the death of Brian Sicknick to push their narrative for impeachment of Donald J. Trump on the charge of inciting the riot. Officer Sicknick was honored with a State funeral that was more sanctimonious political opportunism than any recognition of Officer Sicknick and his family.

The reason for the death of Ashli Babbitt remains unanswered. Her crime of entering the House should not have led to her execution. She had taken an oath to protect the Constitution as an Air Force veteran. She may have thought she was doing just that, and so did thousands of other protestors. Her death by lethal force was an unfortunate mistake in judgement on both sides attributable to the chaos of the moment.

There was a failure in Homeland Security in identifying the pre-planning of radical right-wing organizations with respect to the protests on January 6th. Social media platforms were used to great effect to coordinate the efforts of the militant fringe elements in the storming of the Capitol. The preliminary chatter leading up to the event should have been intercepted by the FBI and the Capitol Police should have been augmented with riot control units of the Washington DC National Guard detachment. City police should have been on standby as well. Both city and Congressional leadership should have had coordinated measures in place to protect the proceedings of a very controversial Congressional session. This was not done.

There were other fatalities during the riot as well. Many of the officials in Congress feared for their lives. This set the scene for militarization of Washington D.C in order to prevent a repeat protest during the inauguration of the President on January 20th. National Guard detachments were sent by every state to the Capitol, seemingly to say that the whole nation was involved with the process of defending the Capitol. The Inauguration was completed without protest, but a significant number of the National Guard units were retained to defend the Capitol grounds and to show the Nation that the Democratic Party was now in command of all government action.

Due to pressure from elected officials, Federal investigative agencies were charged to determine the organizers of the protest and to charge them with a crime which could be as onerous as *sedition*. This investigation would be cheered on by the Democratic party, the mainstream media and Big Tech. This coincided with the desire for many Democrat-elected officials to seek out the names of not only the protestors who forced their way into the Capitol, but also the other peaceful protestors.

"INSURRECTION"

Prior to the Capitol riot, some elected officials to include Representative Alexandria Ocasio-Cortez, requested that Trump administration officials and Trump supporters be put on a list for some sort of punishment to include restricting opportunities for employment. This lack of judgement by the Congresswoman from New York City was unfortunate. Following the riot, Ocasio-Cortez went on social media to say that "she was afraid of being murdered …. there are armed white supremist sympathizers in the Republican caucus." Other Democrats called for removal of the Republican senators who had issued their objections to the electors of some of the States. But those Democrats are challenging the very Constitutional process they took an oath to uphold, and they were wrong to do so. They even forgot their own objections during 2016 election certification.

Now, the preceding synopsis of events is true. The Democratic Party is now in charge of the government of the United States of America. But the power of the government is derived from We the People. The vendetta encouraged by AOC and others was a violation of their oath of office. The near-maniacal vendetta was also being continued by the Speaker of the House, Nancy Pelosi. The second impeachment, this time of a President who had already left office and was not guilty of the alleged crime of inciting a riot against the government, was evil in intent. She would surreptitiously contact the Armed Forces Chief of Staff to discuss the use of Article 25. Her assignment of an unhinged partisan, retired Army Lt. Gen. Russel Honoré, to lead an investigation of the events of January 6th was vindictive and/or irrational. Her continuance as the Speaker should be challenged by all patriots. But there is a remedy for all the Democrat evil being rained down on the American Heartland. It is clearly stated in the Declaration of Independence.

> *"Prudence, indeed, will dictate that Governments long established should not be changed for light and transient causes; and accordingly all experience hath shewn, that mankind are more disposed to suffer, while evils are sufferable, than to right themselves by abolishing the forms to which they are accustomed. But when a long train of abuses and usurpations, pursuing invariably the same **Object** evinces a design to reduce them under absolute Despotism, it is their right, it is their duty, to throw off such Government, and to provide new Guards for their future security."*
>
> The Declaration of Independence (1776)

President Joseph R. Biden Jr. is probably one of the shallowest, most misinformed and least-qualified politicians to ever occupy the Oval Office. He and his VP, Kamala Harris, have no executive experience between them. He has appointed incompetents, racial bigots, and far left zealots to positions where they are now essentially destroying the tenets of the Nation---Equal treatment under the Law, Individual Freedom and Freedom of Speech. Other enumerated Rights are on the chopping block including the Second Amendment. They have set out to destroy their opposition through any means possible, to include means that used to be considered illegal.

The Democratic Party is pursuing the **Object** called **Socialism**. Calling it **Progressivism** does not change what it is. Equity is not Equality. ***Equity is Communism.*** It will lead to Despotism and the loss of the Individual Freedom of all Americans. Many American freedoms have already been revoked. But they can be restored. And they must be restored. It is the Duty of the People to do that by rejecting the Democratic Party and their nearly completed attempt to make the United States a Socialist state. The process to "throw off such Government" is called an **election**, not a revolution or act of sedition. And the remedy that will restore the Values of the American Heartland to all of its People will be the mid-term elections of 2022 and the Presidential election in 2024.

THE RETURN OF OBAMANATION

In 2016, the American Heartland elected a populist President, Donald J. Trump, a Republican. The Republicans also secured a majority in the House of Representatives and the Senate. The reason for this ideological victory was the desire for a change in the elected officials following eight years of economic malaise under the Obama administration.

Nearly all of the Obama administration's policies had been contrary to common sense. It increased taxes and wasted that revenue by doling it out to its major donors which included large corporations that were in process of sending jobs overseas. Obama's policies favored Wall Street, in particular hedge fund managers of all stripes. Artificially low interest rates had been implemented by the Fed and this drove more investment into Wall Street. Simultaneously, the Obama EPA had declared that carbon dioxide was a pollutant and implemented new regulations that would cripple the coal industry and other fossil fuel companies. The Obama administration would be successful in forcing the Nation into a socialized medicine program using a series of unchallenged lies. The resulting Obamacare would place another sixth of the economy under government control.

The Obama administration declared that global warming was an "existential threat" to the United States and the world. Obama entered the nation into the Paris Climate agreement which set unrealistic goals for reducing CO2 emissions by the West while excluding China and India. Only the United States would actually reduce its emissions by switching to natural gas from coal and place the Nation on track to be fully energy independent.

Barack Obama would place his Vice President, Joe Biden in charge of several programs which would fail, such as the 2008 Stimulus investment plan and the reaction to the H1N1 flu response. But Biden would also be placed in charge of high-level diplomacy with Russia, Ukraine and China. This would place him in the position to increase his family's wealth through "plausibility deniability" in his involvement with his son's and brother's dealings with foreign powers. None of this would be revealed until the late stages of the 2020 Presidential campaign and even then, it would be covered up by the media and Big Tech.

Other Obama actions that would also go unseen would involve using the U. S. intelligence operations to spy on the Trump campaign and to set in motion steps to hamstring the incoming Administration under the accusation of "Russian Collusion." The crippled new Administration would still be successful in undoing the mistakes of the Obama years but would rely too heavily on the use of executive action instead of legislative success. The reason for lack of legislative success was primarily the result of the Establishment's success in neutering the President's policies. The Establishment consists of the aged senior politicians in both parties and the Republicans-in-name-only or RINO's. The most powerful Senate RINO's were John McCain, Jeff Flake, Ben Sasse, Susan Collins, Pat Toomey and Lisa Murkowski. John McCain would make a point of being the final vote that stopped the overturning of the worst product of the Obama administration, the Affordable Care Act. Today there are other near-RINO's including many in the House such as Liz Chaney and Mitt Romney in the Senate. While normally rational, they too have let their hatred of Trump cloud their judgement.

There are other problems facing true conservatives today. The support of Trump meant accepting his personality defects in order to advance conservative ideas. The Left would say that was a Faustian bargain, but Trump was no demon, just a man with some human weaknesses. His policies more than offset those weaknesses.

The dream of the Founders of the United States is often cited as being the establishment of a government that would ensure the individual rights of each citizen to Life, Liberty and the Pursuit of Happiness. This can be summed up as the right to Individual Freedom that is protected by a limited government established by the People and for the People. The whole premise of the Nation's Constitution was to limit the power of the government, not to increase it. Even the Founders struggled with that concept during the writing of the Constitution, eventually amending the original document to include a Bill of Rights.

The Bill of Rights is now under attack from forces within the Government and other actors outside the Government. Those outside the Government include Big Tech, the mainstream media, and major corporations. Many of those outside Government are supported by foreign enemies of America.

The external enemies seek the destruction of the United States of America or, at least a reduction in our Nation's status among the nations of the world. In contrast, the enemies within are in pursuit of one thing only, Political Power. With that Power comes status, financial reward and legal protection from wrongdoing.

So Power is the singular goal, even if it means the sacrifice of individual rights and national security. Many elected officials, who took an oath to the protect the Constitution, have betrayed that very oath, and shamelessly so. Some of the betrayals have been due to ignorance of the actual purpose of the Constitution; however, most the betrayals have but one purpose, to remain in control of the lives of individual Americans. This can only be achieved by maintaining the reigns of Political Power through any means necessary. The eventual results justify the means, even if the means are inherently evil. History has shown that even the strongest of nations will first succumb to the Enemy Within, then fall to the Enemy Outside.

Today, the Enemy Within is the senior leadership of the modern Democratic Party and its far-left Democratic Socialist contingent. The former wants to stay in power, the latter wants to gain power. Both see the Declaration of Independence and the Constitution as obstacles.

THE FIVE BIG LIES

The American People are basically good. While this is contrary to some religious beliefs about the inherent internal nature of Humankind, the American Heartland is made up people who desire to get along with each other and to help others when necessary. One word describes the Heartland, that word is **Kindness**. Kindness is found in rural America. It is essentially neighbor helping neighbor in times of hardship and celebrating together when things are good. The American Heartland has only risen to the task in previous generations when the Nation's very existence has been threatened. These past threats have been both external and internal. The external threats have led to wars in foreign lands. The singular internal threat that resulted in war on American soil was the division of the Nation over the institution of Slavery. While Slavery was rejected, the racial bigotry component of that practice continued in the Southern States under the guise of Jim Crow laws and "separate but equal" provisions in state and local laws. This included education where "separate but equal" did not mean equal education outcome. The Nation would not overcome this disparity until the 1960s Civil Rights actions and eventual legislation. All of this progress was resisted by the Democratic party. Today they have convinced the minority population that Civil Rights was the Democratic Party's idea. It wasn't.

The election of an African-American to the Presidency of the United States of America for two terms should have been the signal that racism in America was a thing of the past. But that would have reduced the Democrat claw-hold on Power and the use of Diversity as their rallying cry.

The Democratic Party's success has been built upon Five Big Lies that have had very few challenges from the conservative or truly liberal establishments in Washington DC. Of course, there have been more than five lies in total, but the following five are the foundation of the Democratic Party's success in obtaining control of the Nation through political propaganda, a left biased mainstream media and the censuring of conservative communications by social media platform operators, as well as massive campaign cash contributions from "woke" major corporations.

The Five Big Lies which continue to be espoused are:

1. SYSTEMIC RACISM
2. CATASTROPHIC CLIMATE CHANGE
3. THE GREEN NEW DEAL
4. HEALTHCARE IS A RIGHT
5. CHINA IS NOT OUR COMPETITOR.

But American Heartlanders are not stupid people. They know that they are not racists. They know that resisting open borders is not based on racism, it is the application of common sense. They know that All Lives Matter to God.

They know that Climate Change is not an existential threat to anything. They know that fossil fuels are key to their very way of life.

They know that health insurance is for economic protection from unforeseen major medical problems, not routine healthcare. They know that healthcare decisions are a part of Individual Freedom, not the purview of the State. They know that Obamacare is socialized medicine and that they didn't want it and still don't.

They know that China is our competitor in both economics and ideology. And they know that China cheats in everything they do.

The real question then is, "What is the Heartland going to do about changing the course of the Nation." This is the mission for 2022. It must undo the Big Lies and can only do that through the political process provided by the Founders of this nation— free, fair and honest Elections. The 2022 election is the first battle in the fight which will culminate in the Presidential election of 2024.

BIG LIE NO. 1 "SYSTEMIC RACISM"

The assertion that there is an ingrained racial prejudice in the white majority of American citizens is the basis for the claim of the continued existence of "systemic racism." There are many factors that support the conclusion that a form of racial bias is embedded deeply in the human psyche. Perhaps because it is a natural thing and perhaps, because it can be learned by observation. Racial bias, i.e., prejudice can be reinforced or diminished by a person's environment. No, this is not about Nature and a person's physical environment. This is about human relationships. Most human environmental influencers originate in our relationships with family, friends, associates, competitors and even outright enemies. So, the human mind absorbs all of this influence and reaches a balance of sorts. That balance includes a bias against those who are different. There are many of those types of biases, but racism based on skin color is the bias that is at the forefront of today's social discussion.

The premise that the United States is prejudiced in favor of a white, Anglo-Saxon majority was once true, but it is no longer the case. And it is true that this majority was responsible for 200 years of black slavery followed by 150 years of lightly-veiled bigotry called Jim Crow. But that is over. Even the idea of a white majority is fading. In 2020, non-Hispanic white people, hereafter called whites, are still the majority race representing just under 60 percent of the U.S. population. The white share of the U.S. population has been dropping since 1950 and it will continue to go down. Today, the Hispanic population is the next biggest group at around 19 percent of the U.S., followed by blacks at 13 percent and Asians at less than 6 percent. Only the Hispanic population is increasing. Today, the white population less than 18 years of age is already in the minority.

Eventually, all whites will become a minority, dropping below 50 percent of the U.S. population in 2045. That said, the number of whites with an engrained racial prejudice of any kind is very low and declining. But the old "white racist boogeyman" is still a useful tool for dishonest politicians. They are "gaslighting" the declining white population of the United States into thinking they are evil and deserve to be punished. They are innocent of the charges. But that is what gaslighting is all about, convincing someone of something that is untrue about themselves. Now that is an evil technique and needs to be called out for what it is. Probably the most successful of these gaslighting politicians was, and still is, past President Barack Obama.

FROM CAMBRIDGE TO CHARLOTTESVILLE

The election of the nation's first black president raised hopes that race relations in the U.S. would improve, especially among black voters. But by the end of Barack Obama's second term, and following a spate of high-profile deaths of black Americans during encounters with police as well as protests by the Black Lives Matter movement and other groups, many Americans – especially blacks – described race relations as generally bad.

On July 16, 2009. Harvard University professor Henry Louis Gates Jr., a friend of the new President, Barack Obama, would be arrested at his Cambridge, Massachusetts home by local police sergeant James Crowley, who was responding to a 9-1-1 caller's report of men breaking and entering the residence. The arrest occurred just after Gates returned home to Cambridge after a trip to China. Gates found the front door to his home jammed shut and, with the help of his driver, tried to force it open. A local witness reported their activity to the police as a potential burglary in progress. Accounts regarding the ensuing confrontation differ, but Gates was arrested by the responding officer Crowley and charged with disorderly conduct, (it was reported that Gates wouldn't identify himself).

On July 21, the charges against Gates were dropped. But the arrest generated a national debate about whether or not it represented an example of racial profiling by police. On July 22, President Barack Obama said about the incident, *"I don't know, not having been there and not seeing all the facts, what role race played in that. But I think it's fair to say, number one, any of us would be pretty angry; number two, that the Cambridge police acted stupidly in arresting somebody when there was already proof that they were in their own home, and, number three, what I think we know separate and apart from this incident is that there is a long history in this country of African Americans and Latinos being stopped by law enforcement disproportionately."*

President Obama was both right and wrong. There are more African Americans and Latinos stopped than Caucasians. There are also more African Americans and Latinos incarcerated. Some of the stops are certainly due to racial profiling. The reason is because that is where most of the crime is being committed. The crime rate in New York City was so high in the 1980s and 1990s that the Clinton Administration signed into effect a law sponsored by then Senator Joe Biden called The Violent Crime Control and Law Enforcement Act of 1994, commonly known as the Crime Bill. The 1994 Crime Bill helped decrease the rate of violent crime; however, the rate had begun to decline before the bill went into effect. The bill did contribute to the expansion of incarceration, but, once again, most of this occurred in the fifteen years before the bill was enacted. The racial disparity in incarceration rates is due to enforcement of the Anti-Drug Abuse Act of 1986, which created significant differences in sentencing between crack and powder cocaine. Under this bill, a person was sentenced to a five-year minimum sentence for five grams of crack cocaine, but it took 500 grams of powder cocaine to trigger the same sentence. Because crack is a cheaper alternative to powder cocaine, it was more prominent in low-income neighborhoods. Today the predominate illegal drug is fentanyl that is being produced in

China and Mexico and crossing over the U.S. border or coming in via the mail. Online pharmacies from China are also selling this illegal substance. The neighborhoods with the most illegal drug activity are more likely to be predominately Black and Hispanic.

Is that why the black and Hispanic neighborhoods are more crime ridden? That is the real question that must be answered. And it must be answered by blacks and Hispanics, not predominately black race baiters and white social justice reformers. President Obama missed an opportunity to solve the problem since he was blinded by his own prejudices and perhaps, actual experience with systemic racism. As a lecturer on the U. S. Constitution and its "racial justice" inadequacies at the founding of the country, his bitterness is understandable. But that was history, not the state of the nation when he assumed office in 2009.

It is unfortunate that President Trump did not study the mistakes that President Obama made early in Obama's first term. Of course, Obama was shielded from any negative response by the mainstream media. President Trump would never have that type of cover-up support, even from Republicans.

Trump's primary error occurred when he inserted himself in the Charlottesville, Virginia historic monument controversy. The controversy began before 2016 when protest groups in Charlottesville asked the city council for the local removal of Confederate monuments and memorials, including the statue of Robert E. Lee. Other monuments became part of the controversy, including those of Thomas Jefferson due to his ownership of slaves and those of Lewis and Clark for their advocacy of white colonists over Native Americans.

The actual circumstances surrounding this controversy are important since the resulting propaganda would cause two election defeats. A "Unite the Right" rally was set for Saturday August 12, 2017 from noon until 5 p.m. in downtown Charlottesville at Emancipation Park, where Lee's statue stands. Emancipation Park began to fill with people holding white nationalist banners and Nazi flags, many carrying sticks and some carrying handguns or long guns. Those who had come to protest against the Unite the Right rally were also getting there early. Many in those ranks also carried sticks. The counter-protesters were joined by civil rights activists, Charlottesville residents and church members. As they entered the park, the groups began to form up on one side or the other, and words were being exchanged. In the middle of the two groups was a militia force that had begun to form up in the park. They, too, were armed and were clad in camouflage. They wanted to help keep the peace, they said. The groups became restless and pushing and shoving began between the participants. Both sides swung sticks and shot pepper spray at each other as the groups met in the street. Police were in the vicinity but still did not engage the protesters.

The violence escalated, and bottles and rocks started being thrown. Finally, the police declared the assembly unlawful and ". . . quelled the disturbance at that point." After the gathering was dispersed by police, the Unite the Right rally supporters began making their way to McIntire Park, about a mile north of downtown Charlottesville. At 11:52 a.m., Governor Terry McAuliffe declared a state of emergency as scuffles continued in the city's streets. About a minute later, at 11:53 a.m., UVA canceled all campus activities, effective at noon. At 1:19 p.m., President Donald Trump tweeted a call for an end to the violence. *His first mistake.* Shortly after his tweet, a car driven by James Alex Fields Jr. 20, of Maumee, Ohio, a white nationalist, backed down 4th Street at a high rate of speed and into a crowd of counter-protesters, killing a civil rights activist and injuring 19 others. Now the President was party to the incident, no longer the Chief Executive. He would try to correct the record. And this would set up the propaganda war that would ultimately bring down his Presidency.

At 3 p.m., Trump again spoke from his New Jersey golf club, saying, *"We condemn in the strongest possible terms this egregious display of hatred, bigotry, and violence on many sides, on many sides. It's been going on for a long time in our country. ... It has no place in America. What is vital now is a swift restoration of law and order and the protection of innocent lives. No citizen should ever fear for their safety and security in our society. And no child should ever be afraid to go outside and play or be with their parents and have a good time. ... We must love each other, respect each other and cherish our history and our future together. So important. We have to respect each other. Ideally, we have to love each other."*

In an exchange with reporters at Trump Tower on the Tuesday following the Saturday the rally took place, the President said, *"I think there is blame on both sides. You had a group on one side that was bad. You had a group on the other side that was also very violent. Nobody wants to say that. I'll say it right now. I've condemned neo-Nazis. I've condemned many different groups. Not all of those people were neo-Nazis, believe me. Not all of those people were white supremacists by any stretch. Many of those people were there to protest the taking down of the statue of Robert E. Lee. So this week, it is Robert E. Lee. I noticed that Stonewall Jackson is coming down. I wonder, is it George Washington next week? And is it Thomas Jefferson the week after? You know, you really do have to ask yourself, where does it stop?"*

Later, the President issued the following statement:

"Racism is evil, and those who cause violence in its name are criminals and thugs, including the KKK, neo-Nazis, white supremacists, and other hate groups that are repugnant to everything we hold dear as Americans."

To say that President Trump did not condemn the instigators of violence is Orwellian Doublespeak. But truth doesn't seem to matter to Democrats, including the former First Lady. Mrs. Obama said in a 26-

minute video touting Democratic candidate Joe Biden that *"Republicans are stoking fears about black and brown Americans, lying about how minorities will destroy the suburbs, whipping up violence and intimidation. And they're pinning it all on what's been an overwhelmingly peaceful movement for racial solidarity."* She is referring to the Black Lives Matter movement and Antifa riots plaguing Democrat run cities throughout 2020. She continued: *"Research backs it up, only a tiny fraction of demonstrations have had any violence at all. So what the president [Trump] is doing is once again patently false, it's morally wrong. And yes, it is racist. But that doesn't mean it won't work."* **The real falsehood here is from Mrs. Obama.** The BLM/Antifa riots were violent, buildings were destroyed, minority businesses were ruined, government offices were attacked, and police and civilians were killed.

The fuel that ignited the protests was the death of George Floyd, a black. He was arrested for passing a counterfeit twenty in Minneapolis. While having consumed a lethal dose of fentanyl, he died in police custody. During the arrest he was constrained by a white officer using a knee on Floyd's neck for over eight minutes. On video, it appeared to be excessive force, perhaps even murder and triggered the national protests. Over 20 people were killed, police officers were assassinated, and over 2,000 police were seriously injured. Racism does work, especially in Democrat hands. They call Democrat racism Diversity. And it worked very well along with mail-in balloting to stop the Trump agenda by electing Joe Biden.

The 2020 Presidential election will go down in history as a turning point for the Nation. But the direction of that turn is away from Democracy. It is clear that election laws in several swing states were violated along with Articles I and II of the U. S. Constitution. It is also clear that the U. S. Supreme Court did not perform its duty. Whether these violations and dereliction of duty would have changed the election results is unknown and will probably remain unknown. But it is obvious

BIG LIE NO. 1 "SYSTEMIC RACISM"

that there was a massive protest of Trump supporters at the Capital on January 6, 2021. Most of the protestors were older and white conservative voters, tens of thousands of them. As in the BLM protests all summer that were hijacked by Antifa, this massive protest at the Capital would be hijacked by a few possible far-right elements, some BLM/Antifa infiltrators and some just stupid people. The protest would undo the reason for the protest in the first place. It would destroy the efforts of conservative Senators who were attempting to perform their duty in the Halls of Congress. In this case there would be loss of life. A Capitol policeman would die following the protest and one unarmed female protestor would be shot and killed by a Federal officer.

But once again, the two Obama's and Nancy Pelosi would shout "racism" by saying the white protestors were treated better than an imaginary group of BLM protestors would have been treated. Patently false. No BLM/Antifa vandals were killed by police or Federal agents. But a retired black police officer was killed by Antifa while he was defending a friend's property. Two protestors were killed by a young man defending himself after being attacked by BLM/Antifa thugs during a riot in Wisconsin. He has been unfairly charged with murder.

The United States of America is now the least racist nation in the World and the most tolerant with respect to race, color, creed, and sexual orientation. It is still the most welcoming nation for refugees and other immigrants.

Martin Luther King Jr. had it right, it is the quality of one's character, not the color of one's skin that matters. And Dr. King had the nation on the right track even after his assassination, but the nation went off the rails during the Vietnam War protest era. Protests against the War merged with the Black Panthers movement. This led to a renewed segregation of sorts by blacks themselves as evidenced by an energized NAACP and the growth in political power of the Black

Caucus in Congress. Equal Opportunity in both employment and education had the reverse effect. Dr. King issued a warning in his famous "I Have a Dream" speech on August 28, 1963.

> *"But there is something that I must say to my people, who stand on the warm threshold which leads into the palace of justice: in the process of gaining our rightful place, we must not be guilty of wrongful deeds. Let us not seek to satisfy our thirst for freedom by drinking from the cup of bitterness and hatred. We must forever conduct our struggle on the high plane of dignity and discipline. We must not allow our creative protest to degenerate into physical violence. Again and again, we must rise to the majestic heights of meeting physical force with soul force. The marvelous new militancy which has engulfed the Negro community must not lead us to a distrust of all white people, for many of our white brothers, as evidenced by their presence here today, have come to realize that their destiny is tied up with our destiny, and they have come to realize that their freedom is inextricably bound to our freedom. We cannot walk alone.*
>
> *And as we walk, we must make the pledge that we shall always march ahead. We cannot turn back. There are those who are asking the devotees of civil rights, 'When will you be satisfied?' We can never be satisfied as long as the Negro is the victim of the unspeakable horrors of police brutality. We can never be satisfied as long as our bodies, heavy with the fatigue of travel, cannot gain lodging in the motels of the highways and the hotels of the cities. We cannot be satisfied as long as the Negro's basic mobility is from a smaller ghetto to a larger one. We can never be satisfied as long as our children are stripped of their selfhood and robbed of their dignity by signs stating for whites only. We cannot be satisfied as long as a Negro in Mississippi cannot vote and a Negro in New York believes he has nothing for which to vote. No, no, we are not satisfied and we will not be satisfied until justice rolls down like waters and righteousness like a mighty stream."*

Dr. King raised awareness throughout the country to racial inequality and was given the Noble Peace Prize in 1964 for using nonviolent resistance. Dr. King was not seeking Diversity. He was seeking equality and the integration of his people into America. He did not seek equity in outcome. He was for equality in opportunity. Dr. King was adamantly opposed to self-segregation and its focus on visible differences such as skin color.

> *"I have a dream that my four little children will one day live in a nation where they will not be judged by the color of their skin but by the content of their character."* ----**DR. MARTIN LUTHER KING JR.**

Now, the rules of Diversity require that one's skin color be considered in the scheme of all things. That is not what Dr. King's Civil Rights campaign was all about. It is the direct opposite. It should be "DIVERSITY DOESN'T MATTER." That, of course, leads to the alternative, Meritocracy and that may have its own negative effects. But successful entrepreneurs do not succeed because of diversity or meritocracy. They succeed because of Individual Freedom, perseverance, and the desire to be the best in what they do. Couple those elements with religious freedom and you have defined the value system of the American Heartland.

In the Introduction to her book, *Racism and anti-Racism in the world: before and after 1945,* author Kathleen Brush says: ". . . America was at the fore in 1945. It became the first nation to establish an anti-racist legal system, and then the first nation with a private sector demonstrably committed to anti-racism. It remains at the fore of the demonstrably anti-racist nations." (Brush, 2020)

Today, the United States of America is the least racist nation in the World. The former President, Barack Obama was wrong to use the falsehood of "Systemic Racism" for political gain and has done and continues to do great damage to the Nation. His reversal on "Reparations," is about as weaselly as it gets. The former president claimed that a reparations proposal *did not* make its way through the lawmaking process during his presidency due to *"the politics of White resistance and resentment."* But Obama opposed reparations during his 2008 presidential campaign, arguing that *"the best reparations we can provide are good schools in the inner city and jobs for people who are unemployed."*

President Joe Biden used the lie of Charlottesville to launch his political campaign. He is proud of that fact. *In truth, he should be ashamed.*

But Michelle Obama did say something we can all agree on. *"The work of putting America back together, of truly repairing what is broken, isn't the work of any individual politician or political party. It's up to each of us to do our part. To reach out. To listen. And to hold tight to the truth and values that have always led this country forward. It will be an uncomfortable, sometimes painful process. But if we enter into it with an honest and unwavering love of our country, then maybe we can finally start to heal."*

But this isn't going to happen if the path taken by the Biden Administration continues. **You can't love one half of the country and hate the other half.**

BIG LIE NO. 2 "CATASTROPHIC CLIMATE CHANGE"

Once again, we have the effect of Obamanation. As Chief Executive, Barack Obama bought into the idea that climate change was an "existential threat" to humanity and that the cause was the use of fossil fuels. His successor, Donald Trump, did not buy into the hype. He even called the idea a "Hoax." President Trump was correct, but he didn't do the work necessary to expose the truth in the matter. He could have but he missed multiple opportunities to expose the "Hoax." The idea that climate change is an existential threat is basically idiocy or fraud on a grand scale. So, let's begin by discussing the truths of the matter.

CLIMATE TRUTHS

There is no climate catastrophe. An average global temperature increase of less than 1.5 °C over a period of 100 years will have no adverse effect on human flourishing. It will probably help.

There is no catastrophic effect on the climate due to the use of fossil fuels.

CO_2 plays a very small role in the climate. Water vapor and clouds are much bigger factors.

The minimal heating effect of CO_2 is a good thing for nearly all life on the planet. Humans flourish at warmer temperatures.

Higher CO_2 levels are good for plant growth.

Storms are not getting worse or more frequent due to the increase in CO_2 levels. In fact, the opposite has occurred. While storms may appear to be getting worse, they aren't. There is just more reporting on storms today and more people have moved into harm's way. Storm frequency has actually gone down significantly.

Wildfires have not been increasing due to the increased CO2 levels. Wildfires have declined globally for the last several years. The recent wildfires in California and Australia have been largely due to poor forest management practices, mis-guided environmental constraints on power companies, normal climatic variations in average rainfall, and arson.

The rise in sea level is not accelerating. It is rising at the same rate per year since the end of the Little Ice Age. The rise is trivial and humans have been successfully adapting to it for centuries.

Artic summer ice is increasing again. The polar bear population has grown significantly for the past several years.

The Paris Agreement will increase the emissions of pollutants from coal-fired power plants in China, India and Japan. There will be no noticeable effect on the average global temperature. There will be a dramatic increase in the cost of energy world-wide with no benefit to the climate.

And the biggest truth of all, fossil fuels are good for humanity and the planet. We should keep using them until a more cost effective and reliable energy source is developed which will most likely be nuclear, which is not even a renewable source. Nuclear energy will be so dense that it will not need to be renewable. Solar and Wind Power systems are not reliable or renewable. They require fossil fuels for fabrication, installation, baseload power and rapid back-up power. The actual operational life and final disposal costs for solar and wind installations are already proving to be untenable in Europe.

The large-scale combustion of coal that started the Industrial Revolution in the mid-19th century was the beginning of the release of substantial amounts of CO2 into the atmosphere. Coal has been joined by petroleum and natural gas at an increasing rate in the modern era. Consequently, there has been a steady increase of atmospheric CO2, from around 285 ppm (parts-per-million) in the 1860s to slightly over 400 ppm today. While there may be natural factors in play, there is an increase in CO2 levels due to the burning of fossil fuels. It is unclear how much is attributable to fossil fuels. It may be as high as 50 percent. But so what? The increase has been beneficial.

Gasoline prices increased considerably during the Obama administration until the growth of hydraulic fracturing and directional drilling provided large amounts of shale oil and gas. The path to energy independence was underway in spite of the administration's push for unreliable "renewable" energy sources, solar and wind. Unfortunately, nearly all of the renewable energy sources would rely on manufacturers outside the United States, primarily China. Attempts at solar panel manufacturing in the U. S. would fail, even those supported by massive cash infusions and other subsidies. The Chinese communists could care less about environmental hazards associated with renewable energy. In fact, they increased their construction of coal-fired plants. China knows how to build coal plants. It is the world's largest consumer of coal, drawing more than 70 percent of its electricity from coal, some of that from the U. S. through circuitous means. India is not far behind the Chinese in the construction of coal-fired power plants and they are increasing their use of LNG for domestic use as well.

The climate is affected by many factors and it is always changing. The changes are usually very slow, to the point of being imperceptible to human beings in most cases. The term slow is important here. Slow is a relative term, it is based on a time frame. The forecasts of a pending climate catastrophe play on the human propensity to think in the short time, perhaps less than a generation or so. And this is the whole crux of the catastrophic climate change argument.

Geological time and the physical thermodynamics of scale are important. For example, the heat absorption capacity of the oceans is enormous. It would take millennia for additional heat to be transferred from the oceans to the atmosphere. According to my good friend, geologist [Andy May](), "The true 'control knob' of long-term temperature change is the oceans. They regulate the surface temperatures through their enormous heat capacity. The mixed layer alone has over 22 times the heat capacity of the whole atmosphere up to 22 km. The regulation of atmospheric temperatures by the oceans also gives us a lot of time to determine if global warming is truly a threat. Currently, we only have about fifteen years of ocean temperature data, but in fifteen more years we will have data over a 'climatic' period. If the ocean warming trend in 2035 is still less than one degree per century, we have very little to worry about." Andy May is right. We have time to [adapt to the changing climate](). I wrote a fairly length post on this once.

And climate change can be as much good for humankind as it is detrimental to the human living condition. History shows that humankind adapts to climate change more rapidly than the climate actually changes. It always has. It is our technology, our industrial know-how and affordable, reliable energy that allows us to cope with Nature.

The use of fossil fuels has been the driver of industrial progress, the most successful contributor to improving the human condition with, perhaps, the exception of the Declaration of Independence and the Constitution. The use of fossil fuels, that is petroleum, natural gas and coal, has made a hostile environment not just tolerable, but even enjoyable.

With respect to the effect on the climate of CO_2 generated by consumption of fossil fuels, I am a skeptic. That is not a bad thing. Skepticism is the primary ingredient of scientific progress. It is defined by the Scientific Method. Now, as a matter of full disclosure, I am not a professional scientist. I am a professional engineer. And I spent a quarter of my lifetime in the field of petroleum production and exploration. I didn't work to destroy the planet then and I still don't. Engineers have a tendency to deal in tangible things and leave the more abstract to our scientific brethren like geologists and physicists. My academic training is sufficient to allow me to discern the difference between fact and bovine excrement. There is a lot of the latter in circulation from supposedly academic research and computer modeling.

Now I do know something about computer modeling, that is, my experience is that "garbage in, garbage out" is a true statement. Unfortunately, that practical truth is being ignored. The claim that our use of fossil fuels is destroying the planet is inherently false, but that misconception is being magnified by a hyperbolic mainstream media of non-journalists. Many of the promoters of the war on fossil fuels have a vested interest in perpetuating the Hoax. They are planning to make it rich in the Carbon offset trading business.

The "journalists" may want in on the action or at least have the opportunity to rub shoulders with these scam artists at cocktail parties inside the Washington DC Beltway. The Hoaxers' target audience is the pandering political profession, not the public. But it is the American public that will pay the price, a very big price, for the climate change nonsense exhibited by the following Big Lie No. 3, The Green New Deal.

BIG LIE NO. 3 "THE GREEN NEW DEAL"

"Stupid is as Stupid Does," --Forrest Gump.

No, this is not a repeat of the Climate Change Lie. This is about the proposed Green New Deal drafted by Alexandria Ocasio-Cortez. This is about replacing Free Market Capitalism with Socialism. Of course, it is dressed up in all things Green, from more "unreliable" renewable energy i.e., solar and wind, to banning fossil fuels for transportation use and electrical power generation, to major re-construction of existing buildings (commercial and residential) with more energy efficient materials and designs. Overall, AOC's Green New Deal is a detachment from reality.

Humankind has survived and flourished in a world beset with hazards. Its survival has been aided by its superior intelligence that allowed humankind to leverage the force multiplier of accessible energy. The sun has always provided the energy base but its areal peculiarities and timing variances have created poor living conditions in most locations. Survival has required the successful harnessing of energy from a source other than direct sunlight. The primary alternative source of energy came from the burning of wood, peat, dung and coal. Other energy sources came from the capture of wind and water flow. This allowed the population to grow.

That was the way it was until the beginning of the Industrial Age. Then humankind learned how to harness the energy of combustion by producing steam, first to drive pistons, then turbines. The initial primary fuel (after wood, dung and peat) was coal, then fuel oil and manufactured gas were added to the mix of carbon-based fuels. In the early stages, the primary benefit was mechanical advantage in production processes. But eventually, the primary end product became electricity, what some call secondary energy. Electricity became the primary driver of technological progress. It provided freedom from manual labor which could then be directed to entrepreneurial thought. This led to scientific research that yielded improvements in living conditions.

Electricity could be produced with mechanical generators rotated by hydropower and steam power. The steam was originally produced by burning fossil fuels, primarily coal. Scientific research then developed nuclear power to provide the steam while new turbines were designed to be powered by natural gas. The increased availability of natural gas due to breakthroughs in drilling and production methods along with its lower environmental effects caused a rapid reduction in the use of coal for electrical generation in the United States. Unfortunately, Nuclear power growth was stagnated by fear and ignorance. Misguided government policies on powerplant emissions accelerated the coal-fired plant declines; however, improvements in emission controls, recently revised government policies and increased world demand have slowed the rate of decline in the use of coal. In fact, China will most likely change that decline in coal use to an actual accelerated increase before 2050.

Photoelectric cells arranged in banks of solar panels can use the available sunlight to effectively produce electricity in some locations. Both international and domestic engineering improvements in wind turbine design have also improved this ancient technology. However, small scale solar and wind generated power today are not economically viable in most locations without government subsidies. In addition, both wind turbines and solar panels provide intermittent, even unreliable power that requires either a means to store energy or a backup power source. The backup source is usually a fossil-fueled, hydroelectric, or nuclear powered generation plant. The most reliable back-up power source is a natural gas-fired, gas turbine plant due to its ability to respond quickly. Coal-fired and nuclear plants are less flexible or efficient. However, the on-site storage provided at a coal-fired plant or LNG storage at a gas-fired plant may allow those plants to outperform gas-turbine plants supplied only by natural gas pipelines in extreme emergencies.

Those are the facts. But facts do not seem to matter when political ideologies enter the mix of energy source discussions. It should be understood though that political ideologies did not initiate the Industrial Age, common sense and entrepreneurialism were the driving forces. The goal was to survive and improve one's lot in life. The economic process that supported the entrepreneurial effort required was, and still is, Capitalism. *But the elimination of Capitalism is the ultimate goal of the Green New Deal.*

The Green New Deal that Alexandria Ocasio-Cortez (a professed Democratic Socialist) introduced in early 2019 aspires to power the U.S. economy with 100 percent renewable energy within 12 years and calls for "a job guarantee program to assure a living wage job to every person who wants one," "basic income programs" and "universal health care," financed, at least in part, by higher taxes on the wealthy.

The Democratic Socialists have formed a coalition to attack their perception of pervasive social injustice. They are using imagined catastrophic climate change as the primary reason for the legislation.

The touted goal of the Green New Deal is to "Dramatically expand existing renewable power sources and deploy new production capacity with the goal of meeting 100% of national power demand through renewable sources." This goal is not achievable. Renewables currently contribute 11 percent to total capacity. Biomass, though renewable (about 45% of total renewables), will increase CO_2 emissions (and black carbon emissions) since they require burning. Solar and wind are

55

BIG LIE NO. 3 "THE GREEN NEW DEAL"

contributing less than 3% to total capacity (in 2017). The maximum contribution of wind and solar will not exceed 20% even if viable and scalable energy storage technologies become reality.

The next stated objective is "building a national, energy-efficient, 'smart' grid. This is a great objective. Might we add that it should also be EMP resistant as well as have a lot of nuclear, clean-coal and natural gas turbine power plant nodes attached. An electromagnetic pulse or EMP can be caused by solar activity or a nuclear blast. Prudence would indicate that the United States electrical grid should be "hardened" to resist such an occurrence.

Next on the list we have "upgrading every residential and industrial building for state-of-the-art energy efficiency, comfort and safety." Hard to argue with this either, except, who is doing the upgrading? Who is paying for the upgrading? If it's me, then what if I don't want to? Another IRS-enforced mandate?

The next goal of the Green New Deal is "eliminating greenhouse gas emissions from the manufacturing, agricultural and other industries, including by investing in local-scale agriculture in communities across the country." The problem with this is that fertilizers including CO_2 itself, are necessary ingredients for local-scale agriculture, not to mention large-scale agriculture. Most of the fertilizer is from carbon-based liquids and gas, transported and even injected into the soil with fossil fuel-driven equipment. Harvesting equipment is also very fossil fuel-driven. This infrastructure is not going to change much in 10 years, or 30 for that matter. And here we have another conflict between those of anti-GMO and pro-Organic mindset and the unwashed masses who need to eat to survive. Productivity in agriculture is important to farmers. Unfortunately, some have bitten into the biofuel apple.

As we continue with this legislative punch list, we have "eliminating greenhouse gas emissions from, repairing and improving transportation and other infrastructure, and upgrading water infrastructure to ensure universal access to clean water." While the "eliminating greenhouse gas emissions from transportation" is consistent with the primary goal, it is not clear where "improving other infrastructure including universal access to clean water" comes into play within the scope of the legislation. (Capages, Why the Green New Deal is a Bad Deal for America, 2019)

The rest of the scope of the Green New Deal is essentially spending enough money to put lipstick on this socialistic pig and then try to market it to the world as the latest Made in America fad. China and India are not going to buy into the idea. They need low cost, available and reliable energy. Spain, France, Germany or even the UK are not going to be fooled again. The results of the Green initiatives in California, and even Texas, are beginning to show up as black-outs and rapidly increasing power costs. Californians are used to stupid far-left policies, but Texans are not. Texans are a big part of the American Heartland and will eventually push back on the Green New Deal.

But the elitists have still dragged the United States back into the Paris Climate Agreement. Why? The nonpartisan National Economic Research Associates concluded that "pursuing the Obama/Biden plan to achieve the Paris Climate Agreement would destroy 6.5 million American industrial jobs by 2040. That is why the Trump Administration withdrew from the Paris Agreement in the first place. But the Biden administration has re-entered the Paris Climate Agreement. This is going to cause rising economic damage reaching $2 trillion a year—about $17,000 a household—by 2040. According to Bjorn Lomborg, "The climate impact of all Paris INDC promises is minuscule . . . Even if we assume that these promises would be extended for another 70 years, there is still little impact . . . the entirety of the Paris promises will reduce temperature rises by just 0.17°C (0.3°F) by 2100." It is very unlikely that the Paris Agreement promises will be kept so even this 0.3°F reduction will not be achieved. *So, we will destroy the American economy and achieve absolutely nothing.*

But what about all those "Green Jobs" that will become available? There is no such thing as a "Green Job" in the first place. Solar panels are made in China, wind turbines are built by the existing workforce, not high tech. Installing solar panels on the rooftops is not a high skill tech job. So, when the Green New Deal suggests a massive shift to Green jobs, the media should ask a few questions such as: What is a Green Job? Where will they be found? How do you get trained in such a job?

But every Democrat candidate running for President in 2020 endorsed the Green New Deal, including the eventual successful primary and general election candidate and now President, Joseph Robinette Biden Jr. Biden has appointed the incompetent and Paris Agreement champion, John F. Kerry as the Climate Change Czar, whatever that means. His other appointments are just as bad. But Kerry's position doesn't require Senate advice and consent. John Kerry was a failure as the Secretary of State. He negotiated the nonsensical Iran Nuclear Deal and cost the United States billions of dollars where nothing was gained. He would even undermine the diplomatic efforts of the Trump administration by meeting with Iranian officials, perhaps a violation of the Logan Act. He is not qualified to lead anything. Of course, that doesn't matter.

The Biden Administration is implementing AOC's Green New Deal. They just aren't calling it that.

BIG LIE NO. 4 "HEALTHCARE IS A RIGHT"

No, it is not. The Declaration of Independence includes the phrase, "We hold these truths to be self-evident, that all men are created equal, that they are endowed by their Creator with certain unalienable Rights, that among these are Life, Liberty and the pursuit of Happiness." The Preamble to the U. S. Constitution states "We the People of the United States, in Order to form a more perfect Union, establish Justice, ensure domestic Tranquility, provide for the common defense, promote the general Welfare, and secure the Blessings of Liberty to ourselves and our Posterity . . ." The Declaration defines the rights, the Constitution limits the role of government to one of protection of those rights.

There is no explicit Right to Healthcare. There certainly isn't a mandate that Healthcare insurance must be purchased from anyone, private or public. There is a right to purchase whatever you want to, as long as it is not illegal. That is the Pursuit of Happiness. The role of government is to promote the general Welfare, that means among other things, keeping the economic playing field level and open to all, including the ability to obtain healthcare. Part of "ability to obtain" may be the acquisition of private health insurance, not government healthcare services or government sanctioned healthcare insurance. But when the citizens of the United States implemented Medicare, the "camel got its nose into the tent." In truth, the camel got its nose into the tent with Social Security, but that is ancient history now.

Ask American citizens what they want with respect to healthcare before you delegate responsibility for writing laws to unqualified or compromised bureaucrats. What exactly is healthcare? Let's not ask wealthy Americans about health care. They can afford to get the best regardless. Wealthy politicians like the late Ted Kennedy had no idea what healthcare meant to taxpaying, middle-income America.

BIG LIE NO. 4 "HEALTHCARE IS A RIGHT"

Healthcare for middle-income Americans employed by large and small businesses had been a benefit provided to their employees. The benefit was either provided by making direct payments for healthcare services or by the businesses buying group insurance policies on behalf of their employees. This benefit was considered a competitive tool for attracting and retaining quality employees. Over time, malpractice insurance premiums drove up the cost of both forms of healthcare provision. The group insurance policy costs increased to the point where the employers had to have the employees pay part of the insurance premiums. Since this was usually done as part of the normal payroll deduction process, the effect was often overlooked when payrolls increased.

When the economy started south in 2006, companies started downsizing. People lost their jobs and healthcare benefits. When these displaced employees tried to obtain their own coverage, the actual cost of medical insurance was a shock. Employees with pre-existing conditions were hurt more than anyone. Government-mandated programs which were intended to provide interim coverage were not affordable. The high premiums were again driven by malpractice premiums plus the fact that insurance companies could not compete across state boundaries.

People in a free country with a free-market economy would not consider healthcare benefits a right protected by their constitution. It is a service that can be purchased in the competitive marketplace. When the costs become prohibitive, then medical insurance comes into play. However, insurance providers must also be able to work in the competitive marketplace. Government interference restricts the marketplace to each state, which limits the pool that insurance providers would use to keep premiums down.

Insurance is not purchased for routine items. You don't buy insurance to cover the cost of your groceries. So, you wouldn't buy insurance to cover a routine medical physical. You don't buy insurance to cover the cost of gasoline, but you do buy car insurance. You will probably have a cold or run a fever sometime. It should be up to you if you want to purchase a policy to cover those occurrences. The premiums would be high, since you will have a cold sometime.

What people really want is insurance for catastrophic illnesses or injury that can result in medical expenses that would wipe out the family's fortune. The late Ted Kennedy did not have this problem, so he was not the one to tell the average middle-income and lower-income citizens what they needed. What Congress should have done is ask The People what they wanted first. Then ask the doctors, healthcare industry, pharmaceutical companies and insurance companies how best to fulfill this want. If Congress did this, we must have missed it. It appears that Congress started with their own assumption that The People wanted the government to provide government-controlled universal healthcare. Or, perhaps this was seen as a way to increase government control or influence on our lives. Unfortunately, the latter is the Democratic Party objective.

Lies were told to pass The Affordable Care Act nicknamed Obamacare. They were incredible. "If you like your health plan, you can keep it, period. You can keep your doctor, period. Your insurance premiums will go down $2,500 a year, period." The bill was so complicated, "We had to pass it to see what was in it." And "it would not provide healthcare to illegal aliens or fund abortions." Not only did the ACA force millions of Americans out of health insurance policies they liked — after being promised repeatedly that wouldn't happen — it also subjected tens of millions of families to skyrocketing health insurance premiums and deductibles. Premiums more than doubled from 2013 to 2019, and the average deductible for an Obamacare bronze family plan is now over $15,000— well beyond what most people can afford to spend in the midst of a health care crisis.

Professor Jonathon Gruber of MIT, dubbed the "Architect of Obamacare", said the bill was deliberately written "in a tortured way" to disguise the fact that it creates a system by which "healthy people pay in and sick people get money." He said this obfuscation was needed due to "the stupidity of the American voter" in ensuring the bill's passage. Gruber said the bill's inherent "lack of transparency is a huge political advantage" in selling it. When Gruber was discussing the decision to have the bill tax insurance companies instead of patients, he stated that "the American people are too stupid to understand the difference" between the two approaches. He said the bill passed due to "the lack of economic understanding of the American voter."

Some would say that the actual Architect of Obamacare was Ezekiel Jonathan "Zeke" Emanuel, an American oncologist and bioethicist. Emanuel entered the Obama administration with different views from President Barack Obama on how to reform health care. As a bioethicist, he had written extensively about who should get medical care, who should decide, and whose life was worth saving.

Dr. Emanuel was part of a school of thought that redefined a physician's duty, insisting that it included working for the greater good of society instead of focusing only on a patient's needs. Many physicians find that view dangerous and contrary to the Hippocratic oath. It is essentially Socialized Medicine.

"Emanuel is a technocrat's technocrat who believes that the government that governs health care most governs it best. Toward that end, he wants to erect an all-encompassing medical technocracy in which the federal government, as decided by 'experts,' dictates universal standards of care, establishes prices of physician and institutional compensation, and forces doctors and other health-care professionals to provide controversial services to which they are religiously or conscientiously opposed." (Smith, 2020)

Zeke Emanuel is the classic example of the elitist class that would be in charge of the centralized planning and administration of a national healthcare system. There would be no Individual Freedom with respect to decisions on one's own healthcare, medical decisions, or even your life's remaining value. Your value would depend on your remaining value to the State, not your family, your loved ones or your faith community.

Even after all of these failures with Obamacare, the Democrats continue to say the best way to solve America's health care challenges is to repair Obamacare. The program was defanged when the "Healthcare Mandate" provision was removed by the Trump Administration. But the Democrats used "fixing Obamacare" as their leverage to the successful takeover of the House of Representatives in the 2018 mid-term elections. This strategy caught the Republicans off-guard, and they paid the price. The Trump Administration would be beleaguered by the Russian Collusion investigation and the eventual unsuccessful effort to remove President Trump by impeachment.

Remember President Obama's false claim that Obamacare would *not* provide healthcare to illegal aliens or fund abortions? He said, *"There are also those who claim that our reform effort will insure illegal immigrants. This, too, is false. The reforms I'm proposing would not apply to those who are here illegally."* Then, in a breach of congressional decorum, Republican lawmaker, Congressman Joe Wilson of South Carolina, shouted "You lie." Wilson's shout drew immediate condemnation from both sides of the aisle, ultimately leading him to apologize. He shouldn't have. *What he said was true.*

BIG LIE NO. 4 "HEALTHCARE IS A RIGHT"

In the run-up to the 2020 Presidential campaign, after winning back control of the House in the 2018 mid-terms using the "fixing Obamacare" mantra, the Democratic Party openly campaigned that "they would provide free healthcare to illegal aliens." All of Democrat 2020 presidential hopefuls raised their hands to that effect. Of course, they would change the term illegal aliens to "undocumented immigrants," a typical Democrat maneuver aided by the mainstream media. The open border policy of the Biden Administration is now carrying out that infamous Obama broken promise. Not only are illegal immigrants getting free health care treatments at the border, *they are getting it before the American public does.* They have to be treated quickly of course, since they are going to be released into American communities as fast as they come across the now open southern border. So Big Lie No. 4 includes another lie, "There is no crisis at the Southern Border." As Senator Ted Cruz would say, "Don't believe your lying eyes." There is a crisis and it was caused by the Biden administration, plain and simple.

The problem with Socialized medicine is that it doesn't really work. It always leads to two systems, one for the rich and one for the rest of us. That is what happened in the U.K. and was actually aggravated by the same cause as that happening in the U.S., *an influx of immigrants*, and it is what will happen here. The Practice of Medicine and Healthcare will never be the same.

BIG LIE NO. 5 "CHINA IS NOT OUR COMPETITOR"

"China is going to eat our lunch? Come on, man," said Joe Biden just after announcing his bid for the 2020 Democratic presidential nomination. *"They can't figure out how they're going to deal with the corruption that exists within the system,"* Biden said of China. *"I mean, you know, they're not bad folks, folks. But guess what? They're not competition for us."* The Chinese may not know how to deal with their own corruption, but they sure know how to use corrupt politicians in the U. S. Government and the leaders of major corporations such as the mainstream media, social media or Big Tech, and entertainment industry liberals including the NBA.

In 1992, my fledgling structural engineering company joined the National Federation of Independent Businesses, the NFIB. They sent out a questionnaire soliciting the opinions on the strategic business outlook including future problems ahead. I responded, *"The biggest nemesis for American business is China."*

The Clinton administration had started the transfer of our technology to China in exchange for cash contributions to the Clinton political war chest. Then Senator Biden backed Clinton's deal of letting China into the WTO. The premise was "free-trade." At that time, Biden had backed free trade over his three decades in Congress, during a period when increasing globalization was viewed as a path to prosperity by Washington elitists. He also supported the 1994 North American Free Trade Agreement (NAFTA). As Obama's vice president, he was a vocal proponent of the Trans-Pacific Partnership, the Obama administration's meager attempt to counter China's growing influence in Asia that Biden had actually championed. But China was admitted into the World Trade Organization as a developing country and this

BIG LIE NO. 5 "CHINA IS NOT OUR COMPETITOR"

gained them a real advantage over the United States and the European Union.

My engineering practice thrived until the Democrat takeover of Congress in 2006 and then the economy went into a tailspin. We took our eyes off of the China threat to save the economy and China took advantage of our misplaced focus. So, this is one more of the many errors in foreign policy made by Joe Biden. In his memoir, former Secretary of Defense Robert Gates said, "I think he has been wrong on nearly every major foreign policy and national security issue over the past four decades." I agree. China is our biggest competitor.

According to David Goldberg "China poses a formidable strategic challenge to America, but we should keep in mind that it is in large part motivated by insecurity and fear: America has inherent strengths that China does not. And the greatest danger to America is not a lack of strength, but complacency. China is a phenomenon unlike anything in economic history . . . In an incredibly short period of time, this formerly backward country has lifted itself into the very first rank of world economies." (Goldman, 2018)

The Chinese economy is already bigger than that of the United States. Our economy is still bigger when measured in dollars but the Chinese are gaining on us. But in the next eight to ten years their economy will exceed that of the United States.

China is a "communist" country. The government is based on the devious coercion of unwilling people. The United States became a great nation populated by people who generally chose to be part of it, *if some Native American tribes are ruled out, of course.* China, on the other hand, conquered peoples of different ethnicities and with different languages and has kept them together by force. It is not a truly communist nation since it has a dictator at the top who has been appointed for life. It is Orwell's 1984 with Asian characters.

According to Goldman, "China once covered a relatively small geographic area. It took about 1,500 years for it to reach its current borders in the ninth century. These borders are natural frontiers. China can't expand over the Himalayas to India, while to its extreme west is desert and to its east is the ocean. So, China is not an inherently expansionist power." (Goldman, 2018) *I am not so sure about that.*

"Nor is China unified. It has a written system of several thousand characters that takes seven years of elementary education to learn, working four hours a day with an ink brush, ink pot, and paper. Learning these characters well enough to read a school textbook or a newspaper is how the Chinese are socialized. The current generation is the first where the majority of Chinese understand the common language, due to the centralization of the state and the mass media. But the Chinese still speak very different languages. Cantonese and Mandarin are as different as Finnish and French. In Hong Kong, you'll see two Chinese screaming at each other in broken English because one speaks Mandarin and the other speaks Cantonese and they don't have a word in common. China is inherently unstable because all that holds it together is an imperial culture and the centralized communist party ruling elites and its surveillance organizations, a secret-police on steroids." (Goldman, 2018)

China has undergone many eras of change. From warlords to civil wars followed by starvation, and degradation. The Century of Humiliation, as the Chinese call it, began with the opium wars in 1848 and ended with the success of the Communist Revolution in 1949. That was a century in which civil war claimed untold millions of lives, and the terror of a return to those conditions is a specter that haunts the

Chinese leadership. Future humiliation must be avoided while past humiliation must be avenged. *Look out Japan.*

China, like Russia, responds to its past humiliation by challenging American power. Goldman says, "It would be naïve to expect the Chinese or the Russians to be our friends; the best we can hope for is peaceful competition and occasional cooperation in matters of mutual concern. But it is also important to recognize that American policy errors exacerbate their suspicion and distrust. For example, our decision to impose majority rule in Iraq created a Shi'ite sectarian state now allied to Iran, and it left Iraq's Sunni minority without a state to protect them. This drove the Sunnis into the hands of non-state actors and unintentionally helped al-Qaeda and ISIS. Sunni jihad is a serious security threat to Russia and China, and Russia's intervention in Syria is, in part, a response to our mistakes." (Goldman, 2018)

The Chinese believe in self-control. The Communist party is looked on as a necessary evil. Without this control agent, they believe their society will break down and they will kill one another. They have reason to believe this. The Communist Party dynasty that took charge in 1949 is now riding high in spite of their past failures that cost millions of lives. For the time being, the regime has a great deal of support, even though it is more totalitarian than Hitler or Stalin could have imagined. According to Goldman, "As deplorable as the regime looks to the West, the prospects for transforming China's way of governance to a democracy are slim to none." *So basically, forget it.*

One of the most dangerous misconceptions Americans have about the Chinese is that they can't innovate. We labeled the Japanese the same way after WWII, a big mistake. Made in Japan went from being the label for manufactured junk to being the label for products of the highest quality. The Japanese used just-in-time delivery and Deming's quality control to out-perform everyone.

The Chinese invented gunpowder, the magnetic compass, the clock, and movable type. Their culture is much more conformist than ours, remember, they are communists. While some may think the Chinese are less likely than Americans to be innovators, there are 1.4 billion Chinese, and their research and development (R&D) spending is quickly catching up with ours. They're producing four times as many science, technology, engineering, and mathematics (STEM) bachelor's degrees and twice as many STEM Ph.D.'s as the United States. While only seven percent of U.S. college students major in engineering, in China, that number is nearly 40 percent. *Technology is the key*, but the United States is focused on *"systemic racism."*

At the Biden Administrations first diplomatic meeting with the Chinese in March 2021 in Anchorage, Alaska, Chinese diplomats dressed down Secretary of State Antony Blinken and national security adviser Jake Sullivan. They didn't know what hit them and they were ill prepared. This was a charade for the World audience. China is in a race to achieve global hegemony. It seeks sympathetic World opinion – at least until it has achieved superior military and economic power. That is the touted 2049 goal but the goal posts seem to be closing in.

According to Victor Davis Hanson, "China may have destroyed the culture of Tibet, destroyed democracy in Hong Kong, put Muslim minorities in detention camps and systematically discriminated against African visitors, but the victimizer nonetheless plays the victim of supposed American racism. Each time prominent Americans damn the United States as racist, Chinese racists chime in, "Amen!" So for now, China feigns victimhood, and it seeks solidarity with others inside the United States and abroad who claim to be fellow victims of American racism. Such naked artifice and hypocrisy may seem crazy, given China's atrocious human rights record. But Chinese leaders view our exploding budget deficits, staggering national debt, lax immigration policies, 2020 summer riots and other internal strife as far crazier – and most welcome supplements to their efforts. (Hanson, 2021)

The computing advantage now enjoyed by China is the result of the progressive policies developed by Democrats and lack of oversight by Republicans. This has to change. Second to our erroneous belief that the Chinese are not innovators is our reluctance to notice the massive distortion of the global economic system caused by Chinese industrial and financial policies. The Chinese play dirty. One of the issues raised in the Trump administration's National Security Strategy was that of forced technology transfer. If the U.S. government prohibits the transfer of technology to China, the technology companies of the world will scream, because it will hurt their stock prices. We design the chips, the Chinese steal the design and build the manufacturing plants. This means that we've conceded to Asia, and especially China, the actual manufacturing to the point that we can't put a warplane in the air without Chinese chips. That is both tactically and strategically stupid. China has moved to lock up world resources of rare earth metals used for all types of electronics and electrical motors. We need to counter and do so quickly.

We are in competition with China. We need to continue to innovate but we must protect our intellectual property. And start manufacturing again. We failed to continue this innovation in recent decades. Starting with the Clinton administration, we came to believe we were so powerful that we didn't have to invest in national defense and new technologies. Investment went into the Internet bubble of the 1990s. The markets are closely tied to culture. It is when we have a national security requirement, forcing us to the frontier of physics to develop weapons that are better than those of our rivals, that we get the best kind of innovation. We did this in WWII and in the Space race. So, the government has a critical role in meeting the Chinese challenge.

In his 2015 book, The Hundred Year Marathon, Michael Pillsbury goes to great length to warn American policy makers on the real danger emanating out of China. "Beijing's strategy to replace the United States as the dominant geopolitical power requires America's goodwill and assistance . . . That's one reason China works so hard to shape American perceptions of it . . . the coming decades will be filled not with wars and territorial conquest but rather with struggles over economics, trade terms, currency, resources, and geopolitical alignments." (Pillsbury, 2015)

American leaders need to be wary of personal entanglements with the Chinese. This includes investments and campaign contributions and the continuing swinging door between U. S. government officials and firms lobbying on behalf of China. The perception of corruption is prevalent in Washington today. Too many high-level officials have been compromised by the Chinese to include the President and other senior and junior members of Congress. The Chinese are masters of deception and intrigue. And they plan well ahead, far in advance of Western strategists.

According to Pillsbury, ". . .recognizing that there is a Marathon, may be the most difficult [step] to take, but it is also the most important. America may fail to recognize the problem and may refuse to face the long-term scenario of China not only surpassing us but also growing to double and then triple the size of our economy, by 2049. Then China will have won, by default." (Pillsbury, 2015) In other words, "China is going to eat our lunch."

We can meet the strategic challenge of China, but we have to meet it as Americans in the American way, the smart way, thinking and planning for a Marathon that has a finish line in the year 2049 *or maybe sooner*.

DEFENDING AMERICAN VALUES

The election of Joe Biden as President set the scene for the return of the Obama Administration malefactors and a host of lesser known far-left Cabinet appointments. They will have no opposition since the Senate is now under Democrat control. They will have no opposition in Congress that is. They will be opposed in the Heartland and it will show in the 2022 election first when most patriotic Americans, in particular those in the Heartland, will rise to the occasion and throw the Democrats, along with the RINO's, out of office. But until then, the Biden Administration will do much damage to the Nation. But interestingly enough, the first casualties of Obamanation 2.0 will be the mainstream media. They have been consumed by Big Tech.

THE MAINSTREAM MEDIA

It is clear that today's *Free* Press, the mainstream media, must toe-the-lie and coverup the past corruption of the Biden family, disregard the absolutely feeble mindedness of the Chief Executive, Joe Biden, and downplay the apparent un-preparedness of the Vice President, Kamala Harris, to lead a nation. If they don't, they will be out of favor and join FoxNews on the sidelines. But, they will fall out of favor anyway. That is what happens in a totalitarian state. It is their own creation and they have no one else to blame. It is beyond the dignity of someone the caliber of Anderson Cooper to read Solzhenitsyn and learn what happens to the Press when they become part of the State. They could have a look at Cuba or Venezuela but that might require some work and maybe eating a course of crow or humble pie. Today, the Press is whittling away at its own protection, The First Amendment. They forget that this right was put in place to protect the Press from Government, not to be the Government's henchmen.

DEFENDING AMERICAN VALUES
FREEDOM OF THE PRESS

The First Amendment to the U.S. Constitution reads:

"Congress shall make no law respecting an establishment of religion, or prohibiting the free exercise thereof; or abridging the freedom of speech, **or of the press***; or the right of the people peaceably to assemble, and to petition the Government for a redress of grievances."*

So, what does Freedom of the Press mean today? At the time of the American Revolution, the colonists published a profusion of newspaper articles, books, essays, and pamphlets in opposition to various forms of British tyranny. Thomas Paine's Common Sense (1776) and Thomas Jefferson's Declaration of Independence (1776) are two well-known and influential examples of revolutionary literature published in the colonies. A free press, the Founding Fathers believed, was an essential check against despotism, and integral to advancing human understanding of the sciences, arts, and humanities.

But the Founding Fathers did not agree on how best to protect the press from arbitrary government action. Most favored the English common-law view that equated a free press with the doctrine of no Prior Restraint which meant that no publication could be suppressed by the government before it is released to the public, and that the publication of something could not be conditioned upon judicial approval before its release. But the wrinkle in this was that English Common Law permitted prosecution for libelous and seditious material after publication. Thus, the law protected nasty political publications. It couldn't stop their publication, but the author of the nasty piece could serve time in jail or pay a fine for a wrongful published attack.

A minority view espoused by James Madison felt *"The security of the freedom of the press requires that it should be exempt, not only from previous restraint of the executive, as in Great Britain; but from legislative restraint also; and this exemption, not only from the previous inspection of licensers, but from the subsequent penalty of laws."*

Madison was concerned that authors would be deterred from writing articles that assailed government activity if the government were permitted to prosecute them following release of their works to the public. And he was right. Not only was subsequent punishment permitted for seditious and libelous publications, but in many states, truth was not a defense to allegations of Defamation. If a story tended to discredit the reputation of a public official, the publisher could be held liable for money damages *even if the story itself was accurate.*

This changed in 1964. In the seminal case New York Times v. Sullivan (1964), the U.S. Supreme Court extended First Amendment protection for print and electronic media far beyond the protection envisioned by the English common law. Before money damages can be assessed against a member of the media for a libelous or defamatory statement, the Court held, the injured party, not the publisher, must demonstrate by "clear and convincing" evidence that the statement not only was false but also was published with "actual malice." Actual malice may be established only by proof that the media member recklessly published a statement without regard to its veracity or that it had actual knowledge of its falsity. *Sort of like the Pulitzer Prize winning "Russian Collusion" hoax.* According to the Pulitzer organization, "The New York Times and The Washington Post staff received the award for "For deeply sourced, relentlessly reported coverage in the public interest that dramatically furthered the nation's understanding of Russian interference in the 2016 presidential election and its connections to the Trump campaign, the President-elect's transition team and his eventual administration." *The reporting was a fraud and malicious.*

In Near v. Minnesota (1931), the Court ruled that there is a constitutional presumption against prior restraint that may not be overcome unless the government can demonstrate that Censorship is necessary to prevent a "clear and present danger" of a national security breach. In New York Times v. United States (1971), the Court applied this presumption against the U.S. Department of Justice, which had sought an injunction to prevent the publication of classified material that would reveal the government's secrecy and deception behind the U.S. involvement in the Vietnam War. If this classified material, also known as the Pentagon Papers, had threatened U.S. troops by disclosing their location or movement, the Court said, publication would not have been permitted.

In Bartnicki v. Vopper (2001), the Court confronted an issue involving the privacy of wireless phone conversations and the right of the press to report these conversations. It had to consider whether the government could punish the publication because the information was obtained in violation of the Wiretapping laws. The government had argued that the laws sought to protect the privacy and to minimize the harm to persons whose conversations had been illegally intercepted. The Court ultimately concluded that these privacy interests were outweighed by the *"interest in publishing matters of public importance."* Because the people involved in the intercepted call were public figures, engaged in public matters, they had surrendered some of their privacy rights.

The First Amendment is both simple and complex. But it is clear that the Press is free to report on Government malfeasance without fear of repercussions from the Government or *"public figures involved in public matters."* In fact, the Press has an obligation to do just that. But they haven't. There is a reason for this. It is a new phenomenon that the Founders could not have conceived. The Press is afraid of Big Tech. **They need to be.**

BIG TECH

The power of the multi-billionaire owners and their social media companies on the Internet is beginning to mimic that of the steel and railroad "robber barons" of the early twentieth century. These earlier commodity and manufacturing monopolies were also founded by entrepreneurs. After initial failures and eventual success, these new American capitalists used exploitative practices to amass as significant amount of wealth. These practices included exerting control over natural resources, influencing high levels of government, paying subsistence wages, squashing competition by acquiring their competitors to create monopolies and raise prices, and schemes to sell stock at inflated prices to unsuspecting investors. Sound familiar?

Their downfall began with a mistake by the more famous robber barons, Rockefeller, Carnegie and Morgan. They sought to team up together and help William McKinley win the U.S. presidency in 1896 by making massive contributions to his campaign. With McKinley in their pocket they hoped to avoid an attack on their monopolies. But McKinley was suddenly assassinated, and Vice President Theodore Roosevelt took over. He began dissolving monopolies and trusts in America. In this case, Roosevelt was a true champion of the People.

In 1914 the Federal Trade Commission (FTC) was established as an independent agency of the United States government whose principal mission was the enforcement of civil (non-criminal) U.S. antitrust law and the promotion of consumer protection. The FTC shares jurisdiction over federal civil antitrust enforcement in the United States with the Antitrust Division of the U.S. Department of Justice. The Commission is headed by five Commissioners, nominated by the President and confirmed by the Senate, each serving a seven-year term.

No more than three Commissioners can be of the same political party. The President chooses one Commissioner to act as Chairman.

In 2020, Senator Josh Hawley (R-Missouri) submitted a proposal that goes beyond previous efforts to improve the oversight role of the Fair-Trade Commission, essentially remaking the agency from the ground up. The proposal calls for the FTC to operate within the Department of Justice and be run by a single Senate-confirmed director, rather than its current panel of five commissioners. This would render it more responsive to congressional oversight. Hawley would also establish a "digital market research section" specifically to scrutinize tech platforms.

Alongside those structural reforms, Hawley endorsed a number of legal measures to strengthen the commission, including the power to levy first-time civil penalties and the authority to enforce data portability and interoperability standards. But is that going to fix the real problem with Big Tech? In a Wired.com opinion piece entitled *Should Big Tech Own Our Personal Data?* Steven Hill describes the problem:

> *"Personal data is increasingly a core part of our personhood. Which is why the "service for data" model is a devil's bargain . . . The constant stream of data privacy scandals from Google, Facebook, Twitter, Amazon, and others gives the unmistakable impression that trying to rein in these abuses is like trying to stop water with a net. The US is one of the few developed nations that has no basic consumer privacy law, leaving the Federal Trade Commission with little institutional mandate for enforcement."* (Hill, 2019)

The take-over of personal data has been subtle. It began when Montgomery Ward launched their catalog and mail-order business in the 1870s. Initially, Montgomery Ward mailed unsolicited advertising flyers and one-page catalogs to targeted potential customers living in rural areas and small towns. The business grew and competitors adopted Ward's direct mail tactics. The history is important.

In 1890s, one of Montgomery Ward's largest competitor, Sears and Roebuck had a catalog featuring hundreds of products that was distributed to over 300,000 addresses through-out the United States. The new direct marketing and sales methods used in the mail-order business took advantage of advances in the technology of the times, including improvements in railways and shipping, better postal service delivery, and cheaper printing costs.

Over the ensuing decades, direct mail to targeted customers was followed by telemarketing, broadcast faxing, demographically targeted infomercials, and email spam. Most recently, the industry has evolved into web-based display ads (those awful pop-ups), search engine optimization, and social media targeting. Each technological iteration has allowed ever more gathering of our personal data, as well as more scientific targeting and delivery of advertising, news, and information.

Now, internet-based companies like Google and Facebook have added an entirely new wrinkle to this business model: Instead of charging for their products, they give them away in exchange for vacuuming up our personal data and monetizing it in various ways. Initially this business model seemed benign—beneficial even—because it provided some useful services for free.

But the public is becoming aware of the downsides and hidden costs to this "good deal." Some are mere annoyances, like being constantly tracked by online advertisers. Other downsides are worse; such as facilitating hate speech, leaking personal data, facilitating political targeting, and skewing public discourse through the amplification of "fake news." Personal privacy, societal health, and democratic governance are important. The Sears Roebuck catalog did not attack those ideals. A fundamental shift has occurred.

But perhaps the most significant danger to the Nation that few understand is the "skewing public discourse through the amplification of fake news." Just the term "fake news" is enough for those on the Left to label the ensuing communication as some "far-Right conspiracy theory." But it's not. In fact, the Justice Department recently outlined a proposed overhaul of the legal protections enjoyed by the likes of Google, Facebook and Twitter. The Justice Department proposals would upend these companies' business models by limiting their discretion over removing political posts while also taking away liability protection for encrypted platforms such as Facebook's WhatsApp.

These internet companies currently enjoy immunity, from lawsuits over the content that their users post, under Section 230 of the Communications Decency Act of 1996, a key measure that allowed online companies to flourish in the early days of the internet. Now the provision has become a target of lawmakers from both parties who object to its breadth and describe it as a giveaway to technology companies. The proposal would limit the shield when platforms "purposefully promote, solicit, or facilitate the posting of material that the platform knew or had reason to believe would violate federal criminal law," according to a Justice Department statement. That would include when they receive notice from users or other third parties that the content could be illegal.

The proposed measures would also let victims file lawsuits in cases involving online child exploitation, terrorism, and stalking. They also call for removing immunity entirely if companies cannot identify illegal content and assist in investigating it. Tech companies and civil liberties advocates have said that would hurt services that use end-to-end encryption because finding and tracking such content would be impossible.

While expanding the platforms' responsibility for content, it would also remove their ability to take down content deemed "objectionable," which some conservatives have claimed allows them to silence conservative voices. The claims are true.

Big Tech is fighting the proposed legislation with all their combined might, which is sizeable. Jon Berroya, interim president of the industry's Internet Association trade group that includes Twitter, Facebook and Google, said the Justice Department's proposal *"will make it harder, not easier, for online platforms to make their platforms safe. The threat of litigation for every content moderation decision would hamper IA member companies' ability to set and enforce community guidelines."*

Basically, Big Tech is saying *"Trust us, we will do the right thing."* They like Section 230. In addition to offering liability protection for the content that companies leave up on their sites, Section 230 also allows the companies to remove content or limit its visibility without facing civil liability so long as they act "in good faith." That's the real problem. Their "good faith" leans way left. Tech companies maintain that the shield protects free speech online by encouraging them to leave up controversial content, while also allowing them to take down the most objectionable posts — in essence permitting platforms to let content flourish unimpeded or to police it carefully, as they see fit. Once again, as THEY see fit from their perches on the left.

The companies have argued against almost all changes to the law, saying they would upset this balance and either threaten free speech and innovation on the one hand or limit their ability to take down objectionable content on the other. They have said that liability should attach to speakers, not electronic conduits, and say that their core business models would be at risk if they are forced to face what could amount to billions of lawsuits.

> *"The Trump administration has said we have censored too much content and Democrats and civil rights groups are saying that we aren't taking down enough," Facebook said in a statement. "Section 230 allows us to focus on what matters most: fighting harmful content while protecting political speech."*

But fact are facts and obvious to all. Lawmakers from both parties and critics of Section 230 increasingly say it excuses the Big Tech platforms' worst excesses, with liberals generally arguing for more moderation of election misinformation and racist content and conservatives hoping to change the law to encourage companies to leave up more right-wing voices. Both sides have also slammed the tech companies for what they say is their failure to police drug sales, online child sexual abuse and other ills, saying that it's cheaper for them to ignore the problems. They have also criticized language allowing the shield in U. S. trade agreements.

While Section 230 has no bearing on enforcing criminal law against the platforms themselves, it is largely silent on how the companies should act regarding users who are breaking the law. The recommendations to limit Section 230's protections when companies purposefully facilitate or solicit third-party content that violates federal law, for instance, would clarify that relationship in a way that expands the platforms' legal responsibility and exposes them to more lawsuits.

Courts have generally had to find that platforms contributed materially to illegal content before treating them as responsible for it — such as a website that edited posts to introduce or amplify defamation.

Websites that were set up to attract illegal activity have benefited from the shield, although in 2018, a broad bipartisan majority of lawmakers passed a law removing the protections for companies that knowingly facilitate sex trafficking.

The Justice Department's proposal also seeks to ensure Section 230 wouldn't impair federal civil enforcement, including much of the antitrust and consumer protection law overseen by the U.S. Federal Trade Commission, although it doesn't cite examples where the defense has been used successfully.

BIG TECH ATTACK ON FREE SPEECH AND FREEDOM OF THE PRESS

In October 2020, just prior to the Presidential election, the New York Post published an article on Hunter Biden's emails that indicated he had arranged a meeting with a top Burisma adviser and his father Vice President Joe Biden in 2015. The email correspondence refuted Joe Biden's claim that he had *"never spoken to my son about his overseas business dealings."* The information was recovered from a laptop computer that had been left for repairs but not picked up by the repair company's client, Hunter Biden. [The laptop is now in the hands of the FBI.] The New York Post then distributed the article by posting it on social media. It was big news, and it was based on fact.

Following the post, Facebook announced it was limiting distribution of the New York Post article. Attempts to post the article to Twitter were blocked with a message saying, "We can't complete this request because this link has been identified by Twitter or our partners as being potentially harmful. Visit our Help Center to learn more." The Post's Sohrab Ahmari, responded, *"This is a Big Tech information coup. This is digital civil war. I am editor at The New York Post, one of the nation's largest papers by circulation, can't post one of our own stories that details corruption by a major-party presidential candidate, Biden."* But Twitter would exhibit even more power.

DEFENDING AMERICAN VALUES

The Big Tech censorship was successful. Most of the Democrat and Independent voters on election day knew nothing of the Biden family corruption. They found out later that, indeed, Hunter Biden was the subject of multiple FBI investigations. But the power grab by Big Tech would continue. Congressman Billy Long of Missouri would comment: *"Ayatollah Ali Khamenei, the Supreme Leader of Iran, has advocated for the destruction of Israel and is directly responsible for the deaths of U.S. troops. The President of Venezuela, Nicolas Maduro, jails and kills dissidents in his country and paints a rosy picture to the public. The Communist Chinese spew propaganda to the world on a platform that cannot even be accessed by its own people. So which platform allows Ayatollah Khamenei, President Maduro, and Communist Chinese propaganda? Twitter.*

Twitter permanently banned a sitting United States President but continues to allows other despots to have a global platform. Not only this, Twitter and other social media platforms are now attempting to control speech by banning conservatives from their platforms. These are American companies doing something that is antithetical to the values outlined in our Constitution; using their immense power to shut down free speech."

It was not only Congressman Billy Long who cited the lockdown of President Trump's social media accounts as something contrary to free speech. In lock step, every major Silicon Valley tech company permanently banned the former President of the United States from its platforms, forever. There was a backlash around the world against this move, even from government leaders ideologically opposed to the United States.

The censorship would drive conservatives to seek another social media platform for communication. Since Google had acquired YouTube, even video media was under Big Tech censorship. The first target was the upstart social media company, Parler. Following the Capitol riot on Jan. 6, 2021, Google Play and Apple removed access to the Parler app and Amazon Web Services booted Parler from its servers with only 24-hours notice. At the time, Parler was one of the fastest growing social media sites on the internet. It is now gone. Perhaps it will return on some other platform.

Amazon accused Parler of "helping to incite the Jan. 6 riots at the Capitol that led to the deaths of five people, including a Capitol Police officer." The actual social media platforms used by the small contingent of rioters were Facebook and Twitter, Parler had essentially no role in the riot, but that didn't matter.

The next Big Tech targets would be their enemies in the Senate, in particular, Senator Josh Hawley, the freshman senator from Missouri. Senator Hawley would face the abuse of the social media giants and the Establishment which now included the CEOs of many major corporations. In fact, one of the largest publishers, Simon and Schuster opted out of their contract to publish Senator Hawley's book, *"The Tyranny of Big Tech,"* a book critical of big tech corporations including Google and Facebook, which was set to publish in June 2021. Simon & Schuster would issue a statement that read:

> *"After witnessing the disturbing, deadly insurrection that took place on Wednesday in Washington, D.C., Simon & Schuster has decided to cancel publication of Senator Josh Hawley's forthcoming book, THE TYRANNY OF BIG TECH. We did not come to this decision lightly. As a publisher it will always be our mission to amplify a variety of voices and viewpoints: at the same time we take seriously our larger public responsibility as citizens, and cannot support Senator Hawley after his role in what became a dangerous threat to our democracy and freedom."*

But that is a false statement and based on a misinterpretation of the events of January 6, 2021 in the joint session of the Congress. Senator Hawley has become a target, not for his participation in following the

U. S. Constitution on January 6, 2021, but because he is exposing the corruptive actions of Big Tech. But Senator Hawley is a patriot and a hero to the American Heartland. And both sides of the prevailing politics need to recognize that fact and join Senator Hawley in the breakup of Big Tech before it is too late. It is in their own best interests as well as the Nation's.

> *"If Big Tech's capabilities are allowed to develop unchecked and unregulated, these companies will eventually have the power not only to suppress existing political movements, but to anticipate and prevent the emergence of new ones. This would mean the end of democracy as we know it and place us under the thumb of an unaccountable oligarchy."* (Bokahari, 2021)
>
> ----*Allum Bokhari*

So, now perhaps you understand why Big Tech plowed millions of dollars into the Biden-Harris campaign. They want to stay in charge of your life. With the completed take-over of the Presidency and Congress, it is unlikely that Senator Hawley's legislation will see the light of day. But his book THE TYRANNY OF BIG TECH will be published by Regnery Publishing, the country's leading publisher of conservative books. And perhaps, the notoriety of Simon & Schuster's decision will help in the sales of his book. I hope so.

FREE SPEECH

The right of Free Speech precedes Free Press in the Constitution. Without Free Speech, a Free Press has nothing to offer. So, let us go back to that First Amendment once more:

The First Amendment to the U.S. Constitution reads:

> *Congress shall make no law respecting an establishment of religion, or prohibiting the free exercise thereof; or abridging the* **freedom of speech**, *or of the press; or the right of the people peaceably to assemble, and to petition the Government for a redress of grievances.'*

Among other cherished values, the First Amendment protects freedom of speech. The U.S. Supreme Court often has struggled to determine what exactly constitutes protected speech.

The following are examples of speech, both direct (words) and symbolic (actions), that the Court has decided are either entitled to First Amendment protections, or not:

Freedom of speech includes the right:

Not to speak (specifically, the right not to salute the flag).

Of students to wear black armbands to school to protest a war.

To use certain offensive words and phrases to convey political messages.

To contribute money (under certain circumstances) to political campaigns.

To advertise commercial products and professional services (with some restrictions).

To engage in symbolic speech, (e.g., burning the flag in protest).

Freedom of speech does not include the right:

To incite actions that would harm others such as "shouting fire in a crowded theater."

To make or distribute obscene materials.

To burn draft cards as an anti-war protest.

To permit students to print articles in a school newspaper over the objections of the school administration.

Of students to make an obscene speech at a school-sponsored event.

Of students to advocate illegal drug use at a school-sponsored event.

While these are just a few of the Court decisions on Freedom of Speech, it is interesting to note the number of those originating from the realm of Academia, in particular the college campuses where free speech itself has become a source of contention. Much of this contention is based on the controversy called "political correctness." Political Correctness is actually Cultural Marxism. It is not from the 1960s. It originated in Germany in 1923. And it is evil incarnate if you believe in capitalism, free speech and Individual Freedom.

Today, these "culture wars" have entered a new phase which began in 2014, when multiple prominent speakers were disinvited from campuses following student protests. Some of these incidents were reactions to an unfortunate number of police shootings of African Americans that gave birth to the Black Lives Matter movement. Around the same time, the terms microaggressions, trigger warnings, and safe spaces became increasingly mainstream, introducing a new vocabulary for defining acceptable limits on speech. Political Correctness has morphed into "Wokeness" and "Cancel Culture." That's what it is. And it is wrong.

Most conservatives believe that "the freedom to hear is an essential condition of the university community and an inseparable part of academic freedom."

> *"So long as the broader culture continues to be so deeply polarized, a resolution to the campus free speech debate in the immediate future seems highly unlikely. Neither position can really accommodate compromise: free-speech absolutism and the utopia of inclusivity leave little room for negotiation. Calls for civility entertain the fantasy that the root problem might magically disappear instead of proposing a practical solution. Perhaps the best one can hope for now is the return to what political scientists call forbearance—a willingness, in the name of preserving democratic practices, to refrain from maximizing one's advantages over one's opponents in ways that could result in their obliteration. Far from appeasing or tempering the warring factions of campus culture, calls for free speech, however understood and defined, seem likely, for the foreseeable future, to feed their rage."*
>
> **Michael C. Behrent**-*Associate professor of history at Appalachian State University*

But this is only the condition of Free Speech on the college and university campuses. There is also the censorship by Big Tech on social media, the outcry of mainstream media broadcasters trying to shut down conservative talk radio and conservative cable news channels, and cowardly publishers cancelling contracts on controversial topics that should be available to the general public.

DEFENDING AMERICAN VALUES
THE RIGHT TO BEAR ARMS

The Second Amendment to the Constitution states: "A well-regulated Militia, being necessary to the security of a free State, the right of the people to keep and bear Arms, shall not be infringed." It is the belief of those in the American Heartland that the individual right to bear arms is incorporated through the Fourteenth Amendment and therefore applies to state and local governments.

The Second Amendment means different things to different people. *"The right of the People to keep and bear arms shall not be infringed."* This right goes all the way back to the Hoplites, Ancient Greek citizen soldiers who provided their own weapons to protect their homes and the city state. They were a trained militia. Of course, the use of personal weapons to protect the family and possessions goes even further back, trained militia or no trained militia.

However, the Founding Fathers also had experience with an overbearing monarch and his occupying forces. So perhaps another intent of the "Second" was to also provide a means of organized public resistance to a dictatorial government. This made sense when the weapons of war were no more than muskets, swords and rudimentary cannon. Public weaponry was a match for the oppressing military force. Today, there is no equivalency. Military hardware is powerful stuff. Even a privately-owned AR-15 is no match for an ancient .50 caliber Browning machine gun, let alone an RPG or Hellfire missile. It would take a trained team of AR-15 (M16) experts, a rifle platoon to be effective. The U. S. military are experts in the effective use of a rifle platoon. Unfortunately, so are the Mexican cartels. It isn't paintball. And it isn't some militia or white supremists playing at war. It is real war on the Southern Border, and it is entering the Heartland.

I get it when I hear people call for a national gun registry. It seems so logical until you wonder if the Chicago drug gangs, Mexican cartels and Islamic jihadists have completed their registrations yet. All properly purchased small arms go through required background checks. It would be pretty easy to enter that info into a national database and "viola," you have a national gun registration of all the law abiders. I guess we'll register the criminals after they kill an unarmed citizen. But then, Kamala Harris will bail them out again. But her boss, Joe Biden is on track to do even more damage. On the anniversary of the Parkland school shootings, he promised that his administration would forever protect innocent Americans from similarly senseless crimes and soon enough, with Democrats holding majorities in both House and Senate, pass "commonsense gun law reforms." *"This administration will not wait for the next mass shooting to heed that call . . . We will take action to end our epidemic of gun violence and make our schools and communities safer . . . Today, I am calling on Congress to enact commonsense gun law reforms, including requiring background checks on all gun sales, banning assault weapons and high-capacity magazines and eliminating immunity for gun manufacturers who knowingly put weapons of war on our streets,"* Biden said. This is nonsense.

America's 'epidemic' of gun violence is not in the schools, but in the streets of mostly Democrat-controlled communities. And if Biden and Democrats really wanted to stem the tide of gun-related violence with a 'commonsense' approach, they'd first go after the guns being carted by *lawbreakers* not those carried by *legal owners*. It's not the Second Amendment to blame for America's gun-related crimes and deaths. It is the culture in the big cities where the nuclear family has been destroyed by Progressivism.

"So *'commonsense gun law reforms,'* are really not commonsense. If Democrats truly wanted to address gun violence in America, they would address the problems of those who choose guns and violence as viable ways of life. They wouldn't seek to regulate the ones who don't need regulation in the first place." (Chumley, 2021)

PREPARING FOR 2022 and 2024

To prepare for future action, it is important to understand what happened in the recent past. Perhaps it would be wise to consider the fundamental decline that led to the loss of the House of Representatives in 2018. Then we should examine the other significant events that led to the 2020 election loss of the Presidency and the losses in the Senate.

For some reason, it is accepted that the party in control of the Executive branch will lose seats at the mid-term election. Data supports that assumption, but the reasons are not clear. However, the Democrats did take the House of Representatives in 2018, placing the worst Speaker of the House in American History, Nancy Pelosi, back in power. (Capages, 2020) They did it by using the old worn-out ploy of *"The Republicans are going to take away your Healthcare."* It wasn't true but that didn't matter. It cost the Republicans control of the House.

2018 HEALTHCARE MISSTEP

Senator John McCain's act of hatred towards Donald Trump drove his vote that prevented the repeal of the Affordable Care Act or Obamacare. All 48 Democrats voted no on the repeal of course. But John McCain was joined by fellow Republicans Lisa Murkowski of Alaska and Susan Collins of Maine. They had previously expressed concern with the GOP's repeal strategy. That was the excuse that McCain used to support his vote against the repeal.

"We should not make the mistakes of the past that has led to Obamacare's collapse, including in my home state of Arizona where premiums are sky-rocketing and healthcare providers are fleeing the marketplace." "From the beginning, I have believed that Obamacare should be repealed and replaced with a solution that increases competition, lowers costs, and improves care for the American people. The so-called "skinny repeal" amendment the Senate voted on today would not accomplish those goals. While the amendment would have

repealed some of Obamacare's most burdensome regulations, it offered no replacement to actually reform our health care system and deliver affordable, quality health care to our citizens. The Speaker's statement that the House would be 'willing' to go to conference does not ease my concern that this shell of a bill could be taken up and passed at any time". Senator John McCain

But Senator John McCain was wrong. And his trust in Nancy Pelosi was misguided. And it is also wrong to say the Republicans didn't have a replacement plan for Obamacare. The "replacement" was always there and still is. But, just like the Democrats, the Republicans don't know that either. They have allowed Progressivism to "stick its nose under the Republican tent."

The replacement is called the **private sector.** The real solution is to return healthcare to **We the People** and let the private sector provide competitive healthcare, medical services and health insurance. The only role for government is to ensure price transparency, restrict the formation of monopolies, and oversee standards in medical practice, pharmaceuticals and insurance. And one other thing, medical costs could be reduced considerably if the Democratic Party fifth column, the Trial Attorneys lobby could be defanged with Tort Reform.

The American People do not want, need or desire Socialized Medicine. American business does not want Socialized Medicine. Healthcare insurance was a means to attract employees and maintain company loyalty. The companies were far better than government at providing healthcare *until Medicare requirements and malpractice suits drove up prices.* So, the lesson from the 2018 loss of the House is to *not campaign on reforming Obamacare.* **Campaign on returning Healthcare to the private sector.**

2020 MISSTEPS

Now, let's examine the reasons for the 2020 losses of the Executive Branch and the control of the Senate. There were several events that were not foreseeable as late as December 2019. There were other tragic events that allowed already existing negative forces to move to the media front pages, pushing positive economic and diplomatic successes to the rear, out of public view.

THE COVID 19 PANDEMIC

Most people would say that the loss was due to the COVID 19 Pandemic and the "ineffective management of the ensuing crises by the Executive Branch." The Pandemic certainly had an effect. It provided a means for Nancy Pelosi to implement the Democrat master plan of using mail-in balloting to subvert the electoral process. She did this at the same time as the partisan impeachment of the President on false charges. It also allowed the mainstream media to showcase the principle personality defect of the Chief Executive, Donald Trump's narcissism. It also opened the door for career Establishment operatives to be disloyal to the Chief Executive and undermine Administration successes in handling the crises.

President Trump took near immediate action to shut down the entry of Chinese into the U. S. He was called xenophobic and racist by the media and the Democratic Party. But he saved thousands of American lives. His action was perceived as a bigotry towards Asians, so Nancy Pelosi encouraged people to visit San Francisco's famous China Town. She even took a throng of her followers and the Press to the area. It was pure political theater. It is what she does best.

The Democrats would even find fault in Trump's belief that the origin of the virus was China. This made him a racist according to Pelosi and Schumer. But China had indeed lied about the outbreak and had punished doctors and journalists who told the truth. And the World

PREPARING FOR 2022 and 2024

Health Organization was complicit in the coverup. WHO Director-General Tedros Adhanom Ghebreyesus opined that if "it weren't for China, the number of cases outside China would have been very much higher." In late January, Tedros would even praise Chinese officials for "the transparency they have demonstrated." The corruption was evident to all but the anti-Trump media. Without China's deceit and WHO's coverup on their behalf, the outbreak might have been more limited, and the world at the very least would have had more time to react to the virus. In effect, China and the WHO had worked together to expose the rest of the world to the virus, at the same time they downplayed its dangers while cornering the market on PPE.

It was President Trump's own ego that placed him in the precarious position of taking center stage at the COVID 19 press briefings. The White House Press Pool was not there to serve the public. It was there to torpedo any Trump successes by launching barrages of "gotcha questions" at an easy target. There were some serious reporters who were overshadowed by the showboating elitist reporters of the "fake news" outlets dominated by CNN.

But there was one subject where it is not the President, but the Press Pool that has blood on their hands in addition to the World Health Organization, the FDA and CDC. That subject was hydroxychloroquine, a proven anti-malaria drug that was shown to have therapeutic value and could have saved lives. But it was not sanctioned by the FDA and the World Health Organization, on the basis of a bogus report in Lancet, a UK medical publication. Democrats and the White House Press corps reacted negatively towards the potential use of hydroxychloroquine to save lives due to the Lancet report but *primarily because the drug was touted by President Trump*. As a result of the drug being removed from the list, it worsened the position of hospitals and pharmacies that had refused to use or fill prescriptions on the lifesaving

94

drug. Dr. Ronald R. Cherry, a pulmonary specialist in Tennessee believes that "as many as 200,000 American lives could have been saved if common sense had prevailed from the beginning. A cocktail of Hydroxychloroquine 400mg daily for 7-14 days + Zinc gluconate 50mg daily could have helped our communities avoid the worst of this COVID-19 epidemic and spared our hospitals much grief."

Later on, the WHO was forced to admit that the study they had relied on, which caused them to remove hydroxychloroquine from a list of COVID-19 therapies for further study, *was entirely fictional*. They have now restored the drug to the list. Its effectiveness is now well-established and the fake study worked against tens of thousands of non-trial cases of the drug working to cure COVID-19. It was the failure of the Press to investigate that led to the unnecessary deaths of tens of thousands of COVID-19 patients including nurses, doctors, first responders and essential workers in the U. S. It is clear that "Fake News" can kill.

Trump's best weapon in the fight against COVID 19 could have been the former American ambassador, Dr. Deborah Birx, a physician and diplomat. But she would be overshadowed by Dr. Anthony Fauci and the President himself. Dr. Fauci was a physician-scientist and immunologist. He became director of the NIAID in 1984 and made contributions to HIV/AIDS research and other immunodeficiency diseases, both as a scientist and as the head of the NIAID. From 1983 to 2002, Dr. Fauci was one of the world's most frequently-cited scientists across all scientific journals. *He is a career bureaucrat.*

Dr. Birx's government career started in the 1980s, when she was in the Army and Army Reserve, ultimately reaching the rank of Colonel. During this time, she frequently worked at the Walter Reed Army Medical Center but also spent time in the lab of Dr. Fauci at the National Institutes of Health. They were and still are friends and colleagues. Her reputation was based on her work fighting AIDS, first at the CDC, and later as the US Global AIDS coordinator, where her work was widely praised. That reputation earned her a prominent place in the nation's response to the COVID-19 pandemic, with Trump naming her the Coronavirus Response coordinator and giving her an influential place along with Dr. Fauci on the White House's Coronavirus Task Force.

The White House Press Pool would work to pit the main Response team players against themselves, using President Trump's need to be "front and center" on a subject beyond his expertise. Only Dr. Birx would work to implement logical courses of action that would ease the Nation's panic that was beginning to build in the public at large. She would attempt to undo misstatements by the President without causing him embarrassment. Unfortunately, Dr. Fauci had no compunction to defend the President and would increase the tension with contrary statements to the anti-Trump media outlets. The situation was compounded with the addition of Dr. Scott Atlas to Trump's list of advisors.

Dr. Atlas is an American radiologist, political commentator, and a senior fellow at Stanford University's Hoover Institution, a conservative think tank. From 1998 to 2012 he was a professor and chief of neuroradiology at the Stanford University Medical Center. He is not an epidemiologist. He is just a very smart, non-political practical guy. Atlas was selected by President Donald Trump in August 2020 to serve as an advisor on the White House Coronavirus Task Force. In that role, he was accused of spreading misinformation about COVID-19. He wasn't. He was stating facts. He suggested that face masks and forced social distancing (lockdowns) were not effective in slowing the spread of the coronavirus. He pushed for a faster reopening of schools and businesses during the COVID-19 pandemic and opined that keeping the schools closed was more damaging than the virus exposure risk. As a result, Atlas would be pitted against Fauci and Birx and be labeled as a disrupter along with the "spreading misinformation" claim.

To the media and establishment, it appeared that Atlas had run over Dr. Birx but had been successfully resisted by Dr. Fauci who told the Washington Post, *"I have real problems with that guy . . . He's talking about things that I believe he doesn't have any real insight or knowledge or experience in. He keeps talking about things that ... [don't] make any sense."* Basically, Atlas was a straight shooter who was saying things Trump antagonists didn't want to hear. He would be turned on by the media and his peers in Academia. Such was the reward for service under Donald J. Trump. But the Governor of Florida, Ron DeSantis, would listen and act responsibly, contrary to the "experts." He would handle COVID and the election. He would prove that Dr. Atlas was correct.

But Dr. Fauci would survive. He would be rewarded for his nefarious candor by the next Administration while Dr. Birx would be punished for her honesty and loyalty. She would err by appearing to not follow her own advice about Thanksgiving gatherings and then participating with Dr. Fauci in discrediting the former President. But she was a real National heroine along with the many first responders, nurses and doctors who served in harm's way during the worst early stages of the pandemic.

All of this political theatre would not undermine the real effort against the disease, Project Warp Speed, the development of vaccines to fight the virus. President Trump would go with his strength, the Private Sector and use the logistics expertise of the military as well. New records in vaccine development would be set. In this, the most important part of the whole process to defend the Nation, President Trump would have ultimate success, but of course, no recognition. Nancy Pelosi and Joe Biden would make sure of that.

PREPARING FOR 2022 and 2024

MAIL-IN VOTING

Nancy Pelosi would launch her attack on Individual Freedom and the Bill of Rights as her first order of business in January 2019. It would be called the **For the People Act of 2019**. It would be a direct assault on the American Heartland.

Summary: H.R.1 — 116th Congress (2019-2020)

All Information (Except Text)
There are 2 summaries for H.R.1.
Bill summaries are authored by CRS.
Passed House (03/08/2019)

For the People Act of 2019
AKA The Corrupt Politician's Act of 2019

This bill addresses voter access, election integrity, election security, political spending, and ethics for the three branches of government.

Specifically, the bill expands voter registration and voting access and limits removing voters from voter rolls.

The bill provides for states to establish independent, nonpartisan redistricting commissions.

The bill also sets forth provisions related to election security, including sharing intelligence information with state election officials, protecting the security of the voter rolls, supporting states in securing their election systems, developing a national strategy to protect the security and integrity of U.S. democratic institutions, establishing in the legislative branch the National Commission to Protect United States Democratic Institutions, and other provisions to improve the cybersecurity of election systems.

This bill addresses campaign spending, including by expanding the ban on foreign nationals contributing to or spending on elections; expanding disclosure rules pertaining to organizations spending money during elections, campaign advertisements, and online platforms; and revising disclaimer requirements for political advertising.

This bill establishes an alternative campaign funding system for certain federal offices. The system involves federal matching of small contributions for qualified candidates.

This bill sets forth provisions related to ethics in all three branches of government. Specifically, the bill requires a code of ethics for federal judges and justices, prohibits Members of the House from serving on the board of a for-profit entity, expands enforcement of regulations governing foreign agents, and establishes additional conflict-of-interest and ethics provisions for federal employees and the White House.

The bill also requires candidates for President and Vice President to submit 10 years of tax returns.

H. R. 1 was defeated in the Senate.
A new H. R. 1 was introduced in January 2021.

H.R. 1, the For the People Act of 2021 (the bill will be S. 1 in the Senate), was introduced in the House of Representatives on January 4, 2021. Across ten titles, this Act is supposed to make it easier to vote in federal elections, end congressional gerrymandering, overhaul federal campaign finance laws, increase safeguards against foreign interference, strengthen government ethics rules, and more. Most of these reforms would be implemented for the November 2022 general election, with the exception of some redistricting and public financing changes that would go into effect later.

While the 2019 **For the People Act** was defeated, it was cloned and implemented in the battleground States to good success. The new 2021 version may even be passed in the Democrat-controlled Congress and signed into law by President Biden.

So, the first thing that needs to be realized is that *it is likely that the use of mail-in ballots for major elections is going to continue.* Second, what exactly happened in that 2020 vote? Did the suburban woman vote go to the Democrats because of the personality defects of Donald Trump or was it something else? Third, why didn't more black voters follow the lead of sage advisors such as Thomas Sowell, Shelby Steele, Ben Carson, Condoleezza Rice and so many others? Or why not conservative

PREPARING FOR 2022 and 2024

activists such as Candace Owens, Alan Keyes and Larry Elder? Or black conservative politicians like Tim Scott, Allen West, J. C. Watts and others. Why wasn't the outstanding Republican candidate for the Senate, John James elected by black Michigan voters? Fourth, why didn't more Hispanics vote Republican? Fifth, what do the People want now that Healthcare Insurance has become a government entitlement program? Sixth, why did the public accept the Climate Change existential threat argument? Do they even know the role of fossil fuels in the economy? Seventh, what was the actual impact of mainstream media and social media bias and what can be done about it?

So, what can we do? Raise a white flag and surrender to the far Left? That is not what the American Heartland does. It never has and never will. Let's start by looking at the first challenge, **Mail-In Voting**.

And so the question is, *why is this an advantage for Democrats?* To even ask that question out loud will ignite a firestorm from the mainstream and social media. To them just suggesting that acts of fraud or even irregularities occurred in the Nov. 3rd presidential election will elicit digital shouts that these are baseless claims or unproven. Actually, there are many examples of potential voter fraud that took place during the 2020 election, and serious evidence of voting irregularities relating to the mail-in ballots. To prepare for the elections of 2022 and, in particular, the Presidential election of 2024, the problems need to be examined and corrected at the state level. The following is what actually happened:

> *The State of Nevada rushed a universal vote-by-mail measure through the legislature in response to the COVID-19 pandemic. The bill, known as AB 4, lacked safeguards to assure voter identity and was implemented without cleaning voter rolls of deceased voters, those who had moved, or who had become ineligible to vote. In Senate testimony it was revealed that nearly 90,000 fraudulent or improper votes were cast.*

100

In the State of Wisconsin, there is evidence that over 200,000 ballots that were cast in the state's two most heavily Democratic counties — Dane and Milwaukee should have been disqualified. There were allegations that missing information on absentee ballot envelopes was filled in by unsupervised clerks and still others were the subject of ballot harvesting.

In the State of Michigan there were allegations of problems with voting systems and the software used throughout the state. In addition, in the Detroit, Republican poll watchers were denied access for proper ballot monitoring due to alleged COVID-19 concerns.

In the State of Pennsylvania, Philadelphia election officials denied Republican poll watchers adequate access into counting rooms, requiring them to seek a court order. In addition, over 200,000 more votes were cast than there were voters who voted.

In the State of Georgia there were many irregularities. A video appeared to depict news media and poll watchers being ushered out of the counting room in an Atlanta tabulation center. After all but a few workers left, suitcases of what appear to be ballots were removed from underneath a table and were run through machines. Georgia failed to use signature verification and other measures to certify mail-in ballots.

However, the most contentious issue was the indiscriminate violation of both State and Federal election laws. The Elections Clause of the Constitution, Art. I, § 4, cl. 1, provides that "[t]he Times, Places and Manner of holding Elections for Senators and Representatives, shall be prescribed in each State by the Legislature thereof; but the Congress may at any time by Law make or alter such Regulations. The Clause is a default provision; it invests the States with responsibility for the mechanics of congressional elections), but only so far as Congress declines to pre-empt state legislative choices. Unless Congress acts, Art. I, § 4, empowers the States to regulate.

Thus, it is well settled that the Elections Clause grants Congress "the power to override state regulations" by establishing uniform rules for federal elections, binding on the States. [U. S. Term Limits, Inc. v. Thornton, 514 U. S. 779, 832-833 (1995)]. "[T]he regulations made by Congress are paramount to those made by the State legislature; and if they conflict therewith, the latter, so far as the conflict extends, ceases to be operative." [Ex parte Siebold, 100 U. S. 371, 384 (1880).]

But state and local officials in at least four states — Wisconsin, Michigan, Pennsylvania, and Georgia bypassed their state legislatures and used the COVID-19 pandemic to make last-minute changes to their state voting laws. As already stated, the U.S. Constitution provides that only each state legislature may set the time, place, and manner of elections. That is why Texas Attorney General Ken Paxton filed a lawsuit against the four states with the United States Supreme Court for allegedly exploiting "the COVID-19 pandemic to justify ignoring federal and state election laws and unlawfully enacting last-minute changes, thus skewing the results of the 2020 General Election." Despite the fact 18 more states signed on to Texas' petition, the Supreme Court dismissed the case, citing lack of standing. Only Justices Clarence Thomas and Samuel Alito dissented. *The reluctance of Chief Justice John Roberts and the Supreme Court to take up the matter would lead to the unfortunate events of January 6, 2021.*

It is therefore vary apparent that the primary thrust of preparation for 2022 and 2024 is to take action to ensure election integrity when there is mail-in balloting. **And Mail-in voting is here to stay.** However, with the majority of most state legislatures still under Republican control, passing legislation on improving the validity of the mail-in election balloting process needs to front and center. Eventually, **Mail-in voting will be replaced by on-line voting.** *So, think ahead.*

SUBURBAN WOMEN VOTE

What drove the suburban women vote to the Biden Camp? Easy question to answer, the mainstream media kept the Biden agenda hidden from them and President Trump's offensive tweeting (both uses of the word offensive here) made them feel less secure. The conservative position on Pro-Life versus the left's Pro-Choice may have been a factor as well. Trump is gone now. And the former President needs to stay in the background, supporting Republicans who support his policies, not his persona. President Trump should do some introspection. He once said, the suburban women "must not have liked my personality." Bingo. And the rest of his loyal followers didn't like the tone of his incessant tweeting but understood and agreed with most of his messages. *He should not run in 2024.* He should concentrate on supporting the retaking of the House and Senate in 2022. He should then get behind a strong, less-polarizing candidate for 2024.

The effect of the Biden Administration's leftist agenda will be revealed very quickly as the quality of suburban life declines when inflation starts to take its toll on the suburban life style. The increase in energy costs will be the most visible driving force for rising inflation. That effect should be the primary focus for Republicans. The Pro-Life versus Pro-Choice is not going to be settled at the ballot box. *Stay out of it politically and leave it for the courts to ultimately correct that moral issue.*

THE BLACK EXIT. WHERE WAS IT?

In my second book, Heartland Rebellion, I really thought there would be a major shift of the African American vote from the Democrats to the Republicans. I even called it the Black Awakening. The 2018 election made it clear to me that I was overly optimistic on when the Black exit was going to take place or if was ever going to happen at all. For completeness, the following is what I thought at the time:

"THE BLACK AWAKENING

The predominately black inner cities are beginning to listen to new, conservative black voices. They are now hearing the Truth about the Democratic Party for the first time in nearly a hundred years. Some black celebrities are beginning to question the motives and pandering nature of the Democratic Party. They are starting to suggest that perhaps the black community of regular voters should consider voting for their own interests instead of the real interest of the Democratic Party, remaining in power. The black citizenry has now become over-represented and coddled by the well-intended policies of Affirmative Action and anti-discrimination laws. Major Corporations have dismantled that old scourge of White Privilege. The advertising consortiums and entertainment industry have increased black participation rates well beyond the actual percentages of racial demographics. Old taboos of racial intermarriage, even black LGBTQ relationships, are now made to seem commonplace on the big and little screens. So, with these successes, some of the black celebrities have investigated the reasons for their personal success and pondered the disconnect with their less fortunate brothers and sisters of color. They have discovered the problem quickly. It is their lock-step devotion to the Democratic Party. This will have to change. The leaders of the Black Awakening like Candace Owens and, believe it or not, Kanye West have been viciously attacked by the Left and the Democratic Machine. This has only added more fuel to the Black Awakening."
(Capages Jr., 2018)

I was wrong. There is still only one Republican African American in the Senate, Tim Scott of South Carolina and only two in the House, Burgess Owens and Byron Donalds. A solid contingent, but that is not the sign of a Black Awakening. It is going to take a real effort to identify, recruit and fund a larger number of conservative minority candidates to oppose the Democrats, for example, Herschel Walker in Georgia. The Republican Party should concentrate on the predominately Democratically controlled districts to kick start the Black Exit. The same strategy should be employed for the Hispanic vote as well, but that emphasis should be in Texas as an urgent matter of defense and in California as an offensive measure. It can be done.

HEALTHCARE

Socialized medicine is here, and it is hard to overcome an addiction of this type. Republicans should get some help from the medical professionals and the business community. Leave Medicare alone. Go to work on Tort Reform and setting up Medical Savings Accounts that are 100% deductible from before tax income and are not taxable. Do not limit the percentage of income that can be contributed to these self-directed savings accounts. Allow 100% deductions for catastrophic medical insurance premiums. These steps will allow the People to control their own healthcare.

CLIMATE CHANGE

Climate change alarmism is a religion and based on a perversion of science. It is the means for implementing a Marxist form of government and its inherent elimination of capitalism. Going Green is anti-American dogma. The only good thing about Going Green is that it will not last long when the economic impact becomes apparent. Major utility company commitments to wind and solar projects are going to reduce reliability of the power grid, produce rolling blackouts and drive-up electrical power costs. It will even increase the use of fossil fuels since even solar panel and wind turbine farms need outside power during winter storms. Electric vehicles also need 24/7 available and affordable electricity. That cannot be provided by wind turbines and solar panels, *and never will be*. The Sustainability and Environmental-friendly mantra will still be there, but the People will want their fossil fuels until the only real clean energy future, nuclear power, sheds its fearfully negative image. *Nuclear must be decriminalized and that will take some doing.*

MAINSTREAM MEDIA BIAS AND BIG TECH

The mainstream media has gone off the rails with respect to objective reporting and true journalism. It has actually been supplanted by Big Tech's social media and Big Tech's biased algorithmic control of internet database queries. The solution is straight forward. Break up the monopolistic stranglehold of Big Tech. *Let's have lots of Little Techs.* Then the mainstream media can restore its ethics and burnish the Journalist Creed. There have been too many Pulitzer prizes for poor journalism. It has become far too obvious that today's journalists are not actually journalists, just spineless cretins trying to sit at the popular kids table in high school. They are even using the same crib sheet, repeating each phrase of the day without skipping a beat. *Dust off that Kappa Tau Alpha pledge that originated in the American Heartland and get back to objective reporting.*

DEFENDING THE SECOND AMMENDMENT

The key to maintaining the Right to Bear Arms enshrined in the Second Amendment is to focus the Nation on the real problem, the gun crime in the Democrat-controlled major cities of America.

"You know why there's a Second Amendment? In case the government fails to follow the first one." ---Rush Limbaugh

BUT WHAT ABOUT IMMIGRATION REFORM?

Waves of immigration are usually caused by conditions in the foreign country that result in parts of the populace leaving the country and appearing as refugees seeking asylum. This is different than routine immigration where people are seeking to start a new life to better their economic condition. The former is chaotic and strains the controls at the border. The latter is handled more routinely, "get a number and wait your turn." Since the numbers are controllable, the receiving nation can provide humane and semi-comfortable waiting areas (Ellis Island). The key to the security of any nation is to maintain its borders.

Currently, the Immigration laws are not functional. They have been written to cater to the political benefit of one party seeking more voters and both parties helping major business interests. The need for seasonal migrant labor is declining due to automation in agricultural processes but there is still a market for skilled labor in construction. But today, the driving attractive force for mass immigration is the welfare and education systems of the United States that are paid for by American citizens, not illegal immigrants.

Joe Biden's executive orders to undo the Trump era adjustments to border enforcement and deportations as well as Biden's softer stance with the governments of the Northern Triangle, has now brought a new wave of migrants to the U. S. Border at the worst time possible. Biden's Department of Homeland Security paused deportations for some noncitizens in the United States for 100 days and stopped new enrollments in the Migrant Protection Protocols policy, also known as the "Remain in Mexico" program. This Trump-era policy meant that tens of thousands of people had to wait in Mexico for a chance to get protection in the United States. Now they are waved into the U. S. By stopping the construction of the border wall and hamstringing border patrol with nonsensical rules of engagement, Biden has caused great damage to National security and the U. S. economy.

It is the economics of Immigration that Republicans need to emphasize, not comprehensive reform measures. **To be on offense, the Republicans need to campaign on finishing the Southern border wall for both economic and National defense reasons.**

THE BIG PICTURE

All of the preceding pages of discussion revolve around government policies. That is understandable. This is an ancient problem looking for an answer. The American Experiment introduced the idea of a government by The People and For the People, a representative republic, not a pure democracy. But consider the fact that even a pure democracy could not function without some form of leadership. Decisions must be made. And that is the heart of the problem of government, *any government.*

The People must put their trust in some form of elected guiding council or counselor. A pure democracy would have to rely on an honest vote and then decide on what the results of that vote actually meant. This has evolved into the concept of "the Majority rules." However, the definition of what makes up a majority then comes to the forefront. Does a 51 percent majority represent the Will of the People? *No, it only represents the will of half the People.* The other half are disenfranchised. The American Founders settled on the requirement of two-thirds and three-quarters majorities, but that requirement has been over-ruled many times. It takes work to achieve those kinds of majorities. Work in the form of research, negotiation and compromise, the kind of work that most Establishment politicians avoid at all cost.

A single counselor is dangerous since a dictatorship is always just a hairbreadth away. An elected guiding council would be safer but introduces the concept of corruptive politics and something even more dangerous, rule by elitist oligarchies. And that is where we are in the World today. Nearly all nations are now ruled by elitist oligarchies, including the United States. The controlling powers in Russia, China, and North Korea are obvious oligarchies with dictators at the top with lifetime appointments. The Muslim nations are no different, they just have religious fanatics at the top of the chain of leadership. In the

United States, the oligarchies exist as the cabal of the professional political class called the Establishment, the mainstream media, Academia and globalist corporations, in particular those corporations called Big Tech.

There is a singular underlying cause for the failures in all governments including that of the United States. That cause is unlimited Time in Office. Dictators elected for life is an obvious problem that can only be overturned by some form of revolution. But in America, the solution exists for reducing the Terms of Office of elected officials.

It was spelled out by Thomas Paine in his pamphlet Common Sense as follows:

". . . prudence will point out the propriety of having elections often: because as the elected might by that means return and mix again with the general body of the electors in a few months, their fidelity to the public will be secured by the prudent reflection of not making a rod for themselves. And as this frequent interchange will establish a common interest with every part of the community, they will mutually and naturally support each other, and on this depends the strength of government, and the happiness of the governed."

In other words, short terms in office will make the elected officials more responsive to the needs of their constituency. It will also lower the risk of the formation of a political class aristocracy, The Establishment. Today the Establishment is entrenched. They will not remove themselves. The solution is to amend the Constitution by adding Term Limits. This must be done outside of the control of the Establishment. The procedure to do this is the Convention of States and the mechanism is the Convention of States Project.

PREPARING FOR 2022 and 2024

SUMMARY OF ACTION PLAN
Restore the Cultural Values of the American Heartland

Individual Freedom and Self-Reliance

Equality of Opportunity and Competition

The American Dream and Hard Work

Pass legislation in the States to improve the validity and integrity of the mail-in election balloting process. Push back on H.R.1.

Emphasize the economic destruction of middle-class suburbia and the general American economy by the Biden Administration's war on fossil fuels, immigration enforcement mistakes and its extreme lurch towards Socialism. Support ICE and the Border Patrol. Finish the Southern border wall. Withdraw from Paris Agreement *again*.

Propose privatization of medical healthcare and untaxed, unlimited Medical Savings Accounts. Push Tort Reform legislation in Medicine and Medical Insurance practice.

Make massive increase in identification and funding of Black, Hispanic, and Asian conservative Republican politicians and activists.

Break up the Big Tech monopolies.

Introduce legislation to limit power of public sector unions or make them illegal altogether.

Protect Second Amendment by focusing on inner city Crime.

Support the Convention of States Project.

Refocus on China as our main competitor and plan ahead.

"*That's about it!*" ---- **Bubba Blue in Forrest Gump**

REFERENCES AND WORKS CITED

Bokahari, A. (2021, January). Who is in Control? The Need to Rein in Big Tech. *Imprimis: A publication of Hillsdale College*, pp. 1-5.

Brush, K. (2020). *Racism and anti-Racism in the World: before and after 1945.* Bowker.

Capages Jr., M. (2018). *HEARTLAND REBELLION.* Springfield, Missouri: American Freedom Publications LLC.

Capages, M. (2019). *Why the Green New Deal is a Bad Deal for America.* Springfield, Missouri: American Freedom Publications LLC.

Capages, M. (2020). *PERSISTENT EVIL: SOCIALISM.* Springfield, Missouri: American Freedom Publications LLC.

Cherry, R. R. (2018). *Restoring the American Mind.* Springfield, MIssouri: American Freedom Publications LLC.

Chumley, C. K. (2021, February 16). Biden's 'commonsense gun law reforms' are the lies of the anti-2nd Amendment left. *The Washington Times.*

Epstein, A. (2019, January 12). *Why Green Energy Means No Energy.* Retrieved from industrialprogress.com: http://industrialprogress.com/why-green-energy-means-no-energy/

Goldman, D. (2018, February 21). *How to Meet the Strategic Challenge Posed by China.* Retrieved from imprimis.hillsdale.edu: https://imprimis.hillsdale.edu/how-to-meet-the-strategic-challenge-posed-by-china/

Hanson, V. D. (2021, March 28). *china-contempt-usglobal-hegemony-.* Retrieved from .foxnews.com/opinion: https://www.foxnews.com/opinion/china-contempt-usglobal-hegemony-victor-davis-hanson

Hill, S. (2019, February 13). *Should Big Tech Own Our Personal Data?* Retrieved from Wired.com: https://www.wired.com/story/should-big-tech-own-our-personal-data/

Maryanne Datesman;JoAnn Crandall;Edward Kearney. (2021). *Six Basic American Cultural Values.* Retrieved from https://vintageamericanways.com: https://vintageamericanways.com/american-values/#:~:text=%20History%20Of%20The%20Six%20Basic%20American%20Values,second%20important%20reason%20why%20immigrants%20have...%20More%20

May, A. (2018). *CLIMATE CATASTROPHE: Science or Science Fiction?* The Woodlands Texas: American Freedom Publications LLC.

May, A. (2020). *POLITICS & CLIMATE CHANGE: A History.* Springfield, Missouri: American Freedom Publications LLC.

Pillsbury, M. (2015). *The Hundred Year Marathon.* New York: Henry Holt and Company.

Smith, W. J. (2020, May 12). *Ezekiel Emanuel Wants to Control Your Health Care.* Retrieved from Nationalreview.com: https://www.nationalreview.com/2020/05/ezekiel-emanuel-health-care-policy-joe-biden-administration/

Strassel, K. (2017, April 26). *The Left's War on Free Speech.* Retrieved from Imprimis at Hillsdale.edu: https://imprimis.hillsdale.edu/lefts-war-free-speech/

ABOUT THE AUTHOR

Martin Capages, Jr. is a retired professional engineer, technical executive and an Army veteran. His technical and management experience includes aircraft design, petroleum exploration and production, computer modeling and technology applications and structural engineering. He began writing political commentary in 2009 and completed his first book, *The Moral Case for American Freedom*, in July 2017. His writing is from the perspective of an engineer, Christian layman, conservative and Constitutional originalist.

Martin attended Missouri State University and the Missouri University of Science and Technology where he graduated with a Bachelor of Science in Mechanical Engineering in 1967. After receiving his Commission as an Army Ordnance Officer but prior to reporting for active duty, he joined Boeing Aircraft in Wichita as an Associate Engineer working on the new 737. He reported for active duty in June 1967. After completing active duty, Martin joined Exxon in Houston, Texas, with assignments throughout the U.S. and Europe to include serving as acting North Sea Development Planning Manager for Exxon in London, Production Operations in the Gulf of Mexico, Engineering Manager for the Texas Midland District, the Alaska Financial and Facilities groups, and Exxon's Western Division Computing organization. He left Exxon in 1984 to join Kerr McGee in Oklahoma as Manager of Engineering Services until 1992 when he left the petroleum industry to start his own structural engineering consulting firm, ARIS Engineering Inc., in Springfield, Missouri. He continued post-graduate studies in Civil Engineering and Management receiving an earned Doctorate in Engineering Management in 2002. He retired from full time practice in 2012.

Martin is married to Pamela Kay Capages. They have five children and seven grandchildren. Both Martin and Pamela are active members of their local Baptist church and serve in other state and international Christian ministries. Pamela is an author in her own right and has published books of poetry concerning her Christian faith, family and personal observations of nature.

DISCLAIMER

The material, opinions and positions presented in this book, *HEARTLAND RISING: The Defense of American Values* are those of the Author. The publisher, American Freedom Publications LLC, makes no representations or warranties of any kind and assumes no liabilities of any kind with respect to the accuracy or completeness of the contents of this book.

The author and publisher shall not be held liable or responsible to any person or entity with respect to any loss or incidental or consequential damages caused, or alleged to have been caused, directly or indirectly, by the information contained herein.

OTHER AMERICAN FREEDOM PUBLICATIONS LLC
AUTHOR OFFERINGS

By Martin Capages Jr. PhD

BOOTS TO BOGIES TO BRONZE: The Authorized World War II Biography of 2LT Jack C. Pyatt

THE MORAL CASE FOR AMERICAN FREEDOM

OZARK COUNTY HEART: Boyhood Memories of a Dora Missouri Farm

A WAKEFUL WATCH: The Authorized Biography of Charles Lindbergh Armstrong

HEARTLAND REBELLION

THE SILENT SECOND: The Biography of Martin Capages-Captain USMC

EPIPHANY: Before Time Zero- Faith of an Engineer

WHY THE GREEN NEW DEAL IS A BAD DEAL FOR AMERICA

FREEDOM OR SOCIALISM? The Millennial Dilemma

STARBOARD TACK: The Free Nation Makes a Course Correction

OF OSTRICHES AND LEMMINGS: The Silliness of Climate Change Hysteria

PERSISTENT EVIL—SOCIALISM: A Warning for the Millennial Generation

SHOW-ME WARRIOR O. K. Armstrong of Missouri

By Pamela Kay Capages

POEMS BY PAMELA

WILDWOOD PSALMS

By Ronald R. Cherry MD

RESTORING THE AMERICAN MIND

By Andy May

CLIMATE CATASTROPHE! Science or Science Fiction?

BLOOD & HONOR: The People of Bleeding Kansas

POLITICS AND CLIMATE CHANGE: A History

By Orland Kay Armstrong

OLD MASSA'S PEOPLE: The Old Slaves tell their Story

www.ingramcontent.com/pod-product-compliance
Ingram Content Group UK Ltd.
Pitfield, Milton Keynes, MK11 3LW, UK
UKHW022224230426
12048UKWH00016BA/1047